Warman's

Majolica

Mark F. Moran

Identification and Price Guide

©2005 Krause Publications
Published by

kp books
An Imprint of F+W Publications

700 East State Street • Iola, WI 54990-0001
715-445-2214 • 888-457-2873

Our toll-free number to place an order or obtain
a free catalog is (800) 258-0929.

Library of Congress Catalog Number: 2005906846

ISBN: 0-89689-224-7

Designed by Kay Sanders
Edited by Dennis Thornton

Printed in China

CONTENTS

It Was a Very Good Year

In 1851, California had been the nation's 31st state for only four months, and Millard Fillmore was U.S. president; Elisha Otis was perfecting his brake-equipped elevator, and Robert Bunsen was tinkering with the burner that would one day bear his name; Jenny Lind, the "Swedish Nightingale," toured America in a spectacle organized by P.T. Barnum; Nathaniel Hawthorne's "The Scarlet Letter" was being hailed by critics.

And an English potter was hoping that his new interpretation of a centuries-old style of ceramics would be well received at the "Great Exhibition of the Industries of All Nations" set to open May 1 in London's Hyde Park.

Queen Victoria's husband Albert, the Prince Consort, championed the industrial fair, which was based on French trade events begun in the late 18th century.

Entrepreneur Joseph Paxton came up with plans for a spectacular building made up of nearly a quarter-million panes of glass and a supporting iron framework. When this "Crystal Palace" opened its doors on May 1, 1851, it could hold 60,000 people at one time, in addition to nearly 14,000 exhibits.

American entries included a set of "unpickable" locks, a model of Niagara Falls, a McCormick reaper and a Colt revolver.

There was the Koh-i-Noor diamond (which weighed 787 carats when it was found in India); a knife with 1,851 blades; a prototype submarine; gas cookery, electric clocks, and one of the earliest versions of a washing machine. And then there was the Minton booth.

Potter Herbert Minton had high hopes for his display. His father, Thomas Minton, founded a pottery works in the mid-1790s in Stoke-on-Trent, Staffordshire. Herbert Minton had designed a "new" line of pottery, and his chemist, Leon Arnoux, had developed a process that resulted in vibrant, colorful glazes that came to be called "majolica."

Joseph Francois Leon Arnoux was born in Toulouse, France, in 1816, the son of a porcelain and earthenware manufacturer. Trained as an engineer, Arnoux also studied the making of encaustic tiles, and had been appointed Art Director at Minton's works in 1848. His job was to introduce and promote new products. Victorian fascination with the natural world prompted Arnoux to reintroduce the work of Bernard Palissy, whose naturalistic, bright-colored "maiolica" wares had been created in the 16th century. But Arnoux used a thicker body to make pieces sturdier. This body was given a coating of opaque white glaze, which provided a surface for decoration.

Minton triple-shell seafood condiment server with shell handle, rare form, shape no. 1557, date code for 1870, minor rim chips to shell, 5 1/2" tall, 8" wide, $2,300+

Pieces were modeled in high relief, featuring butterflies and other insects, flowers and leaves, fruit, shells, animals and fish. Queen Victoria's endorsement of the new pottery prompted its acceptance by the general public.

Bernard Palissy (1510-1590) was an artist, writer and scientist, yet he is most celebrated for his ceramics, and for the development of enameled earthenware (also called faience, from the Italian city of Faenza), and for the exuberant plant and animal forms his work took.

Palissy was born in southwestern France. Around 1540, he moved to Saintes, north of Bordeaux, married and set up shop as a portrait painter. Legend has it that he was once shown an earthenware cup (probably of Italian origin), and was so attracted to its tin-based glaze that he decided to devote his time exclusively to enameling, despite having no previous knowledge of ceramics.

The tradition of tin-glazed and decorated earthenware is believed to have originated in the 9th century, somewhere in Persia. These wares moved along trade routes to the island of Majorca, a regular stop for trading vessels traveling between Spain and Italy. When the ceramics were imported into Italy, they came to be called "Maiolica."

Minton Palissy-style platter, professional hairline crack repair to center, 15" wide, $200+

Palissy eventually succeeded in creating brilliant enamel glazes. But after his death in 1590, his work was ignored for centuries.

In the 19th century, private collectors and museums started acquiring original Renaissance pieces, and that helped to revive interest in traditional majolica.

When Minton introduced his wares at Philadelphia's 1876 Centennial Exhibition, American potters also began to produce majolica.

The Griffen, Smith and Hill pottery of Phoenixville, Pa., produced some of the most collectable American majolica from 1879 to about 1893. The company was best known for the manufacture of "Etruscan Majolica" ware. Most pieces are marked with one of the two versions of their crest. However, some unmarked pottery can also be attributed to Griffen, Smith and Hill.

The Chesapeake Pottery in Baltimore, Md., made Clifton, a pattern featuring blackberries and, later, other types of fruit and flowers. This company also made Avalon Faience, a design imitating French faience.

Etruscan conventional cake stand, hard to find, strong color, 10" diameter, 4 3/4" tall, $375+

Other Majolica Makers

John Adams & Co., Hanley, Stoke-on-Trent, Staffordshire, England, operated the Victoria Works, producing earthenware, jasperware, Parian, majolica, 1864-1873. (Collector's tip: Jasperware is a fine white stoneware originally produced by Josiah Wedgwood, often colored by metallic oxides with raised classical designs remaining white.)

Another Staffordshire potter, Samuel Alcock & Co., Cobridge, 1828-1853; Burslem, 1830-1859, produced earthenware, china and parian.

The W. & J.A. Bailey Alloa Pottery was founded in Alloa, the principal town in Clackmannanshire, located near Edinburgh, Scotland.

The Bevington family of potters worked in Hanley, Staffordshire, England, in the late 19th century.

W. Brownfield & Son, Burslem and Cobridge, Staffordshire, England, 1850-1891.

T.C. Brown-Westhead, Moore & Co., produced earthenware and porcelain at Hanley, Stoke-on-Trent, Staffordshire, from about 1862 to 1904.

The Choisy-le-Roi faience factory of Choisy-le-Roi, France, produced majolica from 1860 until 1910. The firm's wares are not always marked. The common mark is usually a black ink stamp "Choisy-le-Roi" pictured to the right with a large "HB." The "HB" stands for Hippolyte Boulenger, a director at the pottery.

Choisy-le-Roi rabbit plate, 8 3/4" diameter, $200+

Jose A. Cunha, Caldas da Rainha, southern Portugal, worked in the style of Bernard Palissy, the great French Renaissance potter.

William T. Copeland & Sons pottery of Stoke-on-Trent, Staffordshire, England, began producing porcelain and earthenware in 1847. (Josiah Spode established a pottery at Stoke-on-Trent in 1770. In 1833, the firm was purchased by William Copeland and Thomas Garrett. In 1847, Copeland became the sole owner. W.T. Copeland & Sons continued until a 1976 merger when it became

Royal Worcester Spode. Copeland majolica pieces are sometimes marked with an impressed "COPELAND," but many times are unmarked.)

Julius Dressler, Bela Czech Republic, company founded 1888, producing faience, majolica and porcelain. In 1920, the name was changed to EPIAG. The firm closed about 1945.

Eureka Pottery was located in Trenton, N.J., circa 1883-1887.

Railway Pottery, established by S. Fielding & Co., Stoke, Stoke-on-Trent, Staffordshire, England, 1879.

There were two Thomas Forester potteries active in the late 19th century in Staffordshire, England. Some sources list the more famous of the two as Thomas Forester & Sons Ltd. at the Phoenix Works, Longton.

Established in the early 19th century, the Gien pottery works is located on the banks of France's Loire River near Orléans.

Joseph Holdcroft majolica ware was produced at Daisy Bank in Longton, Staffordshire, England, from 1870 to 1885. Items can be found marked with "JHOLDCROFT," but many items can only be attributed by the patterns and colors that are documented to have come from the Holdcroft potteries.

George Jones & Sons Ltd., Stoke, Staffordshire, started operation in about 1864 as George Jones and in 1873 became George Jones & Sons Ltd. The firm operated the Trent Potteries in Stoke-on-Trent (renamed "Crescent Potteries" in about 1907).

George Jones chestnut leaf on napkin plate, 9" diameter, $225+

In about 1877, Samuel Lear erected a small china works in Hanley, Staffordshire. Lear produced domestic china and, in addition, decorated all kinds of earthenware made by other manufacturers, including "spirit kegs." In 1882, the firm expanded to include production of majolica, ivory-body earthenware and Wedgwood-type jasperware. The business closed in 1886.

Robert Charbonnier founded the Longchamp tile works in 1847 to make red clay tiles, but the factory soon started to produce majolica. Longchamp is known for its "barbotine" pieces (a paste of clay used in decorating coarse pottery in relief) made with vivid colors, especially oyster plates.

Hugo Lonitz operated in Haldensleben, Germany, from 1868-1886, and later Hugo Lonitz & Co., 1886-1904, producing household and decorative porcelain, earthenware and metalwares. Look for a mark of two entwined fish.

The Lunéville pottery was founded about 1728 by Jacques Chambrette in the city that bears its name, in the Alsace-Lorraine region of northeastern France. The firm became famous for its blue monochromatic and floral patterns. Around 1750, ceramist Paul-Louis Cyfflé introduced a pattern with animals and historical figures. Lunéville products range from hand-painted faience and majolica to pieces influenced by the Art Deco movement.

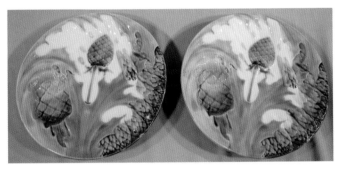

Pair of Lunéville asparagus plates, each 9" diameter, $200+ pair

The Massier family began producing ceramics in Vallauris, France, in the mid-18th century.

François Maurice, School of Paris, active 1875-1885, worked in the style of Bernard Palissy, c. 1510-1590, the great French Renaissance potter.

George Morley & Co., East Liverpool, Ohio, 1884-1891.

Morley & Co. Pottery was founded in 1879, Wellsville, Ohio, making graniteware and majolica.

Orchies, a majolica manufacturer in northern France near Lille, is also known under the mark "Moulin des Loups & Hamage," 1920s.

Faïencerie de Pornic is located near Quimper, France.

Quimper pottery has a long history. Tin-glazed, hand-painted pottery has been made in Quimper, France, since the late 17th century. The earliest firm, founded in 1685 by Jean Baptiste Bousquet, was known as HB Quimper. Another firm, founded in 1772 by Francois Eloury, was known as Porquier. A third firm, founded by Guillaume Dumaine in 1778, was known as HR or Henriot Quimper. All three firms made similar pottery decorated with designs of Breton peasants, and sea and flower motifs.

The Rörstrand factory made the first faience (tin-glazed earthenware) produced in Sweden. It was established in 1725 by Johann Wolff, near Stockholm.

The earthenware factory of Salins was established in 1857 in Salins-les-Bains, near the French border with Switzerland. Salins was awarded with the gold medal at the International Exhibition of Decorative Arts in Paris in 1912.

Sarreguemines wares are named for the city in the Lorraine region of northeastern France. The pottery was founded in 1790 by Nicholas-Henri Jacobi. For more than 100 years, it flourished under the direction of the Utzschneider family.

Wilhelm Schiller and Sons, Bodenbach, Bohemia, established 1885.

Thomas-Victor Sergent was one of the School of Paris ceramists of the late 19th century who was influenced by the works of Bernard Palissy, c. 1510-1590, the great French Renaissance potter.

St. Clement: Founded by Jacques Chambrette in Saint-Clément, France, in 1758. Chambrette also established works in Lunéville.

The St. Jean de Bretagne pottery works are located near Quimper, France.

Vallauris is a pottery center in southeastern France, near Cannes. Companies in production there include Massier and Foucard-Jourdan.

Victoria Pottery Co., Hanley, Staffordshire, England, 1895-1927.

Wardle & Co., established 1871 at Hanley, Staffordshire, England.

Josiah Wedgwood was born in Burslem, Staffordshire, England, on July 12, 1730, into a family with a long pottery tradition. At the age of nine, after the death of his father, he joined the family business. In 1759, he set up his own pottery works in Burslem. There he produced cream-colored earthenware that found favor with Queen Charlotte. In 1762, she appointed him royal supplier of dinnerware. From the public sale of "Queen's Ware," as it came to be known, Wedgwood was able to build a production community in 1768, which he named Etruria, near Stoke-on-Trent, and a second factory equipped with tools and ovens of his own design. (Etruria is the ancient land of the Etruscans, in what is now northern Italy.)

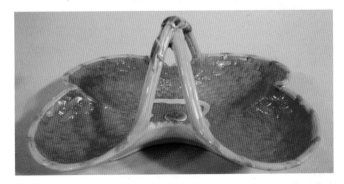

Wedgwood pink basket-weave basket with yellow rim and handle wrapped with green ribbon, rim and handle repair, 8" wide, $150+

How to Use This Book

This book is organized by form, then alphabetically by manufacturer, color or design detail, and includes sections on assorted groupings of majolica, asparagus plates and accessories, banks, baskets, bottles, bowls, busts and figures, butter pats, cachepots, cake stands, candleholders, centerpieces, cheese keepers, comports (or compotes), creamers and sugars, cups and saucers, assorted dishes, eggcups and holders, ewers, humidors, inkwells, jardinières, jugs, match boxes and strikers, mugs, oyster plates and accessories, pitchers, place card holders, planters, plates, platters, plaques, punch bowls, salts, sardine boxes, sauce dishes, servers, shelves, spooners, teapots, tea sets, tiles, toothpick holders, trays, tureens, umbrella stands, vases and flowers holders, wall pockets, and "Other Pieces," including ashtrays, boxes, chandeliers, garden seats, lamps, pen wipes, smoking sets, spoon warmers, string holders, waste bowls, and wine coolers.

(Note: Though many of the pieces here were once intended for use at the dinner table, vintage majolica should never be used to serve or store food because of the lead- and tin-based glazes used in their production. Glazes on contemporary majolica dinnerware are not a hazard.)

Every collecting area has its own language that presents a challenge for beginners. Michael G. Stawser's Majolica Auctions, of Wolcottville, Ind., a dominant force in the selling of majolica, uses both a broad description—"various conditions" for a group of pieces—and specific information on chips, hairline cracks, flaking, crazing and staining. Add to this the factors that determine desirability, like graphic impact, rarity and regional collecting tastes, and you can see how difficult it might be for a group of collectors to be unanimous in their assessment of a given piece of majolica.

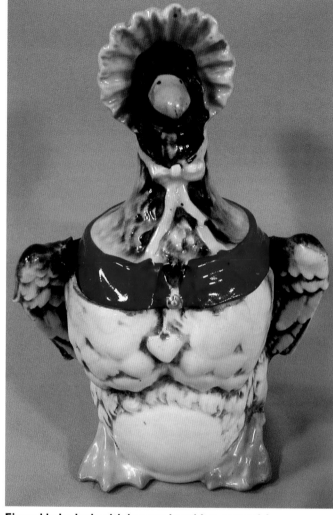

Figural lady duck with bonnet humidor, unusual form, 8 3/4" tall, $450+

Pricing

The prices in this book have been established using the resources in private collections, and with the help of respected dealers and auctioneers. Some majolica collectors have seen dramatic fluctuations in values over the last decade (usually upward, in this collecting area), but a growing number of reproductions have eroded collector confidence, sending prices for certain vintage pieces lower. And like any investment, collections are subject to changes in the wider economy, and to changing tastes.

When comparing your pieces to examples in this book, pay close attention to details like surface wear, rarity and, of course, cracks and chips, all of which can affect value dramatically.

Many prices in this book also include a "+" sign, which indicates that the value may have been established at an auction, and does not include a buyer's premium, usually 10 percent.

Remember: A price guide not only measures value, but it also captures a moment in time, and sometimes that moment can pass very quickly. The old adage, "An antique is worth what someone will pay for it," is just as true for majolica as for other collecting areas. By using this book and other reliable resources, collectors will learn how to get the best examples for their investment.

Words of Thanks

This guide would not have been possible without the help and good wishes of the following folks:
DawnNita Glass, Strawser Auction Group
Joan Sween
Richard and Kae Townsend, the Iridescent House

Reproductions

There is almost no area of antique collecting that is not plagued by fakes and reproductions. For collectors of majolica, the only way to avoid reproductions is experience: Making mistakes and learning from them; talking with other collectors and dealers; finding reputable resources (including books and Web sites), and learning to invest wisely, buying the best examples one can afford.

Beginning collectors will soon learn that marks can be deceiving, labels and tags are often missing, and those that remain may be spurious.

Reproduction Minton fish oyster plate, 10 3/4" diameter, $30+

How does one know whether a given piece is authentic? Does it look old, and to what degree can age be simulated? What is the difference between high-quality vintage majolica and modern mass-produced examples? Even experts are fooled when trying to assess qualities that have subtle distinctions.

There is another important factor to consider. A contemporary maker may create a "reproduction" pitcher or plate in tribute of the original, and sell it for what it is: a legitimate copy. Many of these are dated and signed by the artist or manufacturer, and these legitimate copies are becoming collectible today. Such items are not intended to be frauds.

But a contemporary piece may pass through many hands between the time it leaves the maker and winds up in a collection. When profit is the only motive of a reseller, details about origin, ownership and age can become a slippery slope of guesses, attribution and—unfortunately—fabrication.

As the collector's eye sharpens, and the approach to inspecting and assessing majolica improves, it will become easier to buy with confidence. And a knowledgeable collecting public should be the goal of all sellers, if for no other reason than the willingness to invest in quality.

For a wide-ranging look at the many kinds of reproductions in the marketplace, visit www.Repronews.com.

Repronews.com is the online database of fakes and reproductions. It began in 1992 as the monthly printed newsletter, Antique & Collectors Reproduction News. After more than 12 years of producing the black and white printed edition, the full color database was launched in December 2004.

The online database includes all the past articles plus continuous updates on the latest fakes and reproductions as they are discovered. At the time of launch, the database included almost 1,000 articles and reports with more than 7,000 photos and illustrations. Additional research material is also included such as patents from various foreign countries and an extensive marks library.

Articles are searchable with standard search engine techniques, and can also be browsed by title with an A-to-Z list. Subscribers may print articles for personal use on their home or office computers. Color photos and illustrations will print in color on color printers.

Articles are researched and prepared by repronews.com staff in consultation with leading collectors, dealers, clubs and institutions.

The monthly newsletter was begun by publisher Mark Chervenka, who continues to manage the online database.

Majolica Assortments

The groupings of majolica pieces listed here are representative of what a collector might find at large auction or private sale. Some pieces are grouped by color or pattern, others by use, and a few by manufacturer. The phrase "various conditions" is shorthand for a range of cracks, chips, flaking, repairs, crazing and staining. Rare or important pieces of majolica will usually have a provenance, and any repairs or restorations should be noted when they are sold.

Though assortments may offer limited information on the value of any single piece, they are an excellent place for beginning collectors to start gathering information on makers, marks, years of production and rarity.

Seven assorted pieces
various conditions.

$140+ all

Fifteen small plates
saucers and sauce dishes, various conditions.

$225+ all

Thirteen pieces
Nine plates, two trays, sugar and creamer, various conditions.

$375+ all

Bamboo and bird teapot
and basket-weave and floral basket, both repaired.

$190+ pair

Begonia bowl
begonia pitcher and mottled egg basket, various conditions.

$160+ all

Majolica Assortments

Cobalt butterfly and fan platter
squirrel on cobalt leaf tray and Etruscan maple leaf plate, various conditions.

$325+ all

Cobalt leaf tray
and overlapping begonia leaf low cake stand.

$225+ pair

Eight cobalt items
teapot, fish vase, two plates, sugar, pitcher, cup and comport (compote), various conditions.

$350+ all

Three Continental plates
and one vase.

$150+ all

Five Continental items
including two humidors and three match holders, various conditions.

$150+ all

Six Continental pieces
including three figural vases, figural tray, match striker and pipe-on-leaf tray, various conditions.

$150+ all

Corn pitcher
bowl, floral and leaf tray and saucer, various conditions.

$100+ all

Large corn tankard
four large and two small corn mugs, various conditions.

$300+ all

Etruscan geranium platter
cobalt geranium plate and leaf tray, various conditions.

$250+ all

Ten small cream pitchers
and one mug, various conditions.

$425+ all

Eight Etruscan items
various conditions. (Collector tip: Made by Griffen, Smith and Hill of Phoenixville, Pa., 1879 to about 1890.)

$225+ all

Etruscan pieces
oak leaf tray, maple leaf plate; shell and seaweed, three cups, two saucers, 8" plate, various conditions.

$350+ all

Nine Etruscan items
including several shell and seaweed plates, and one Continental plate, various conditions.

$325+ all

Fourteen Etruscan items
including shell and seaweed motif and others, various conditions.

$450+ all

Twelve Etruscan items
various patterns, pieces and conditions. (Collector tip: Made by Griffen, Smith and Hill of Phoenixville, Pa., 1879 to about 1890.)

$425+ all

Twelve Etruscan albino shell and seaweed items
including two teapots, four pitchers, sugar, cup and saucer, and four plates.

$325+ all

Fifteen Etruscan Classical pieces
including comport (compote), plates, cup and saucer, and sauce dish, various conditions.

$200+ all

Etruscan shell and seaweed
large crooked-spout teapot, shell and seaweed bowl, bamboo cup and saucer, various conditions.

$325+ all

Etruscan shell and seaweed creamer
and two cups, various conditions.

$100+ all

Majolica Assortments

Three face jugs
and one humidor base, various conditions.

$250+ all

Figural fish pitcher
and fish tray, various conditions.

$110+ pair

Figural fox tray
large deep bowl with leaves and ferns, low shell comport (compote), various conditions.

$250+ all

Floral pitcher
shell pitcher and Continental vase, various conditions.

$90+ all

French floral comport
(compote) and wall pocket floral basket, various conditions.

$100+ pair

Thirty-six-piece set
of German turquoise bird and grape pieces including cake stand, platters, bowls, plates, cups, saucers.

$400+ all

Green, yellow and brown
blended umbrella stand and mottled butterfly pedestal.

$225+ pair

Four Hooligan figural items
including two match strikers, vase and planter, various conditions.

$30+ all

George Jones
albino floral and basket pitcher, rim repair, hairline, 6" tall, and Avalon grape-pattern chamber pot with lid. (Collector tip: Avalon Faience made by Chesapeake Pottery in Baltimore, Md.)

$90+ pair

George Jones
porcelain hummingbird and floral wall pocket, hairline cracks, and an Avalon pitcher. (Collector tip: Avalon Faience made by Chesapeake Pottery in Baltimore, Md.)

$25+ pair

Leaf and fern comport
(compote), bird covered cracker box and strawberry plate, various conditions.

$250+ all

Five leaf trays
and dishes, and porcelain oyster plate, various conditions.

$130+ all

Six Massier flowers
Massier three-part server and Massier-type covered lemon, various conditions.
(Collector tip: The Massier family began producing ceramics in Vallauris,
France, in the mid-18th century.)

$30+ all

Eight majolica plates
bowls, and butter pat, various conditions.

$150+ all

Five miniature
Sarreguemines-type face jugs and bottle.

$130+ all

Mottled pineapple tray
and floral platter, various conditions.

$160+ pair

Oak leaf tray
leaf platter, cobalt mug, cup, sauce dish, and peacock vase, various conditions.

$185+ all

Pineapple pitcher
wild rose pitcher, and basket-weave and bamboo teapot, various conditions.

$220+ all

Five pitchers
and two mugs, various conditions.

$275+ all

Three plates
comport (compote), and humidor, various conditions.

$50+ all

Two platters
and one strawberry tray, various conditions.

$575+ all

Two platters
and two bowls, various conditions.

$200+ all

Sanded floral jardinière
and Continental Art Nouveau vase, various conditions.

$120+ pair

Sarreguemines covered
strawberry tureen and cauliflower covered butter tub, various conditions.

$150+ pair

Two teapots
cup and saucer, spooner and mug, various conditions.

$150+ all

Four trays
and one teapot, various conditions.

$130+ all

Wedgwood cobalt
cauliflower comport (or compote) and Wedgwood cauliflower bowl, various conditions. (Collector tip: Founded by Josiah Wedgwood in 1759 at Burslem, Staffordshire, England.)

$300+ pair

Wheat and baskets
match striker and figural swan teapot, age unknown.

$50+ pair

Asparagus Plates and Accessories

Like oyster plates, tableware related to serving asparagus has become a popular collecting area in itself. We know that asparagus has been cultivated for thousands of years, but it wasn't until the Victorian era that inexpensive, mass-produced serving pieces began to take on the forms of their intended use. The whimsical asparagus cradles are among the most popular forms.

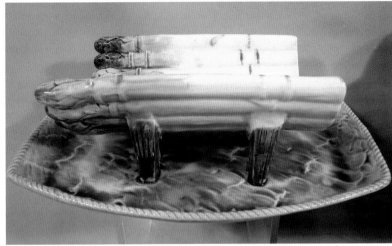

French asparagus cradle
with attached under plate, 11" long.

$225+

French asparagus covered barrel
three piece, with under plate, strong color and detail, tray 14" long, barrel 11" long, 7 1/2" tall, professional repair to leaf on barrel cover.

$800+

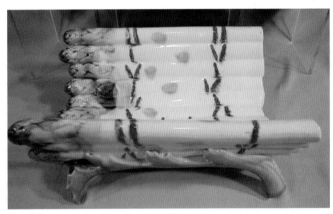

French asparagus serving cradle
strong color, 10" long.

$200+

French wagon asparagus cradle
and matching under plate, unusual cobalt, professional repair to corner of tray, 11" long.

$100+

French asparagus plate
9" diameter.

$125+

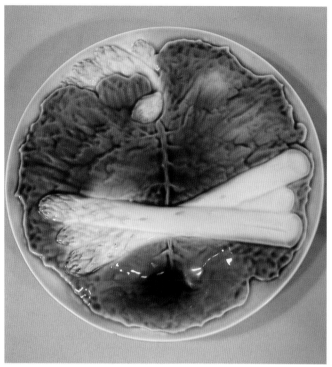

French asparagus plate
9 1/2" diameter.

$175+

French asparagus plate
9 1/2" diameter.

$125+

French asparagus plate
9 1/2" diameter.

$125+

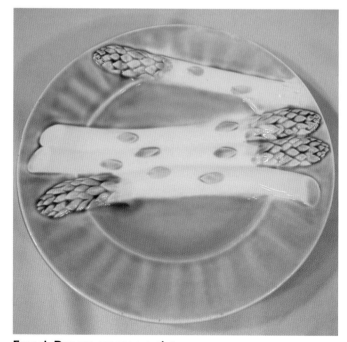

French Depose asparagus plate
8 1/2" diameter. (Collector tip: "Depose" means registered.)

$125+

Pair of French asparagus plates
one stained, each 10" diameter.

$100+ pair

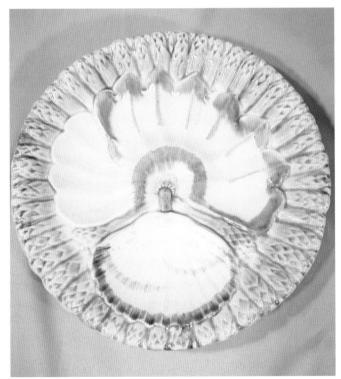

Square Longchamp asparagus plates
pair, each 9 1/4".

$225+ pair

Longchamp asparagus plate
10" diameter. (Collector tip: Robert Charbonnier founded the Longchamp tile works in 1847 to make red clay tiles, but the factory soon started to produce majolica. Longchamp is known for its "barbotine" pieces [a paste of clay used in decorating coarse pottery in relief] made with vivid colors, especially oyster plates.)

$125+

Longchamp French asparagus tray
and cradle, good color, 13 1/2" long.

$250+

Longchamp French asparagus set
eight-piece, with four plates, sauce boat, platter, and platter with cradle.

$900+ set

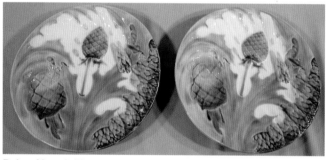

Pair of Lunéville asparagus plates
each 9" diameter. (Collector tip: The Lunéville pottery was founded in 1720 by Jacques Chambrette in the city that bears its name, in the Alsace-Lorraine region of northeastern France. The firm became famous for its blue monochromatic and floral patterns. Around 1750, ceramist Paul-Louis Cyfflé introduced a pattern with animals and historical figures. Lunéville products range from hand-painted faience and majolica to pieces influenced by the Art Deco movement.)

$200+ pair

St. Clement French asparagus plate
9" diameter. (Collector's tip: Founded by Jacques Chambrette in Saint-Clément, France, in 1758. Chambrette also established works in Lunéville.)

$50+

Minton asparagus server
with attached under plate, shape no. 1549, date code for 1874, professional rim repair, 10" long.

$8-$1200

Banks

The figural banks pictured here are only a small sample of the range of shapes and colors that collectors will encounter. Other examples include hard-to-find banks like a tree stump with applied bird and flower, $300+; and even a zeppelin with gondola, $180+.

Brown dog-head figural bank

$30+

Continental face bank
small base nick to back, 3 3/4" tall.

$60+

Baskets

Majolica baskets had a great variety of uses: they held calling cards, potpourri and sweets, but mostly they were just meant to look pretty on a sideboard or parlor table. While their uses seldom contributed to damage or wear, collectors should closely examine handles, floral or figural decorations, and raised bases for signs of repair.

Continental plate
in wire frame basket with wire handle, minor hairline crack to plate.

$40+

Double basket
with bird below twig handle, hairline crack, 11" long.

$110+

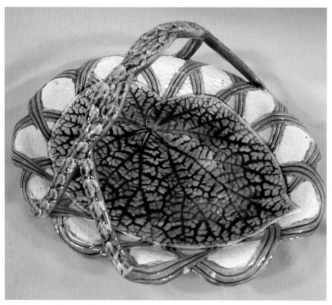

Etruscan begonia
leaf and wicker basket minor professional rim repair to underside, rare, 12" long. (Collector tip: Made by Griffen, Smith and Hill of Phoenixville, Pa., 1879 to about 1890.)

$300+

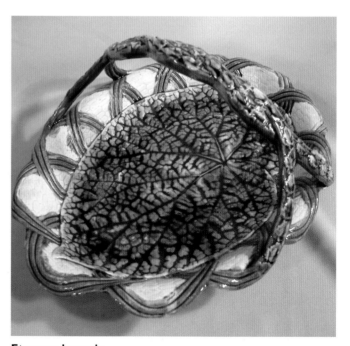

Etruscan begonia
leaf and wicker basket, 12" long.

$400+

Floral and basket-weave basket
with bird perched on twig handle, bird missing beak, 8" tall.

$300+

Holdcroft cobalt
rustic floral strawberry basket with twig handles, professional rim repair, 12" long. (Collector tip: Joseph Holdcroft majolica ware was produced at Daisy Bank in Longton, Staffordshire, England, from 1870 to 1885. Items can be found marked with "JHOLDCROFT," but many items can only be attributed by the patterns and colors that are documented to have come from the Holdcroft potteries.)

$400+

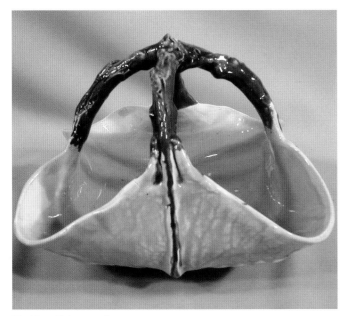

Holdcroft turquoise
tree bark basket with twig handle and feet, hairline crack, rim chip.

$225+

Luggage strap
and floral basket, factory glaze misses to interior of basket, professional repair to handle, 12 1/2" long.

$170+

Sarreguemines fruit basket
strawberry basket and egg basket, and boat-shaped basket, various conditions.

$160+ all

Tree-trunk and knothole basket
9" long, 8" tall.

$300
Courtesy of Joan Sween

Turquoise picket fence
and floral oval footed basket, good detail, rim nick, 6" long, 4" tall.

$70+

Six-sided basket
with ribbon handle and butterflies, unusual, 5 3/4" tall.

$200+

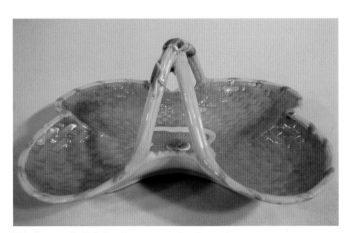

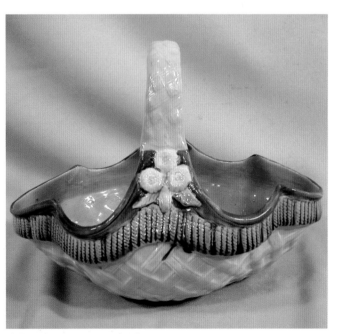

Wedgwood pink basket-weave basket
with yellow rim and handle wrapped with green ribbon, rim and handle repair, 8" wide. (Collector tip: Founded by Josiah Wedgwood in 1759 at Burslem, Staffordshire, England.)

$150+

Yellow basket-weave basket
with flowers, attributed to Holdcroft, 10" long.

$300+

Bottles

Figural bottles like those seen here had a variety of uses, including as liquor flasks and even as cruets for oil and vinegar.

Continental cat
with fish figural bottle, 6 3/4" tall.

$150+

Continental figural pig bottle
nick to ear, 6" tall.

$60+

Continental figural bottle
pig with red smoking jacket, rim chip, 4 3/4" tall.

$130+

Set of four
Continental figural men bottles.

$50+ all

Bowls

Some majolica pieces listed here are valued in groups, and are representative of what a collector might find at large auction or private sale. Some pieces are grouped by color, others by use, and a few by manufacturer. The phrase "various conditions" is shorthand for a range of cracks, chips, flaking, repairs, crazing and staining. Rare or important pieces of majolica will usually have a provenance, and any repairs or restorations should be noted when they are sold.

Though assortments may offer limited information on the value of any single piece, they are an excellent place for beginning collectors to start gathering information on makers, marks, years of production and rarity.

Also see punch bowls.

Continental oval cobalt fruit bowl
Art Nouveau style, 12 3/4" wide, 6 1/2" tall.

$40+

Copeland putti center bowl
cobalt ground, one head broken, 17 1/2" long, 11" tall. (Collector tip: William T. Copeland & Sons pottery of Stoke-on-Trent, England, began producing porcelain and earthenware in 1847.)

$50+

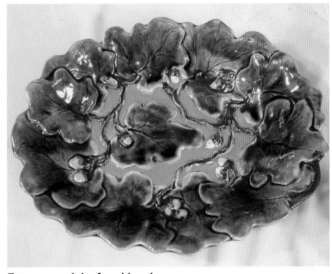

Etruscan oak leaf oval bowl
with pink center, strong color, 12 1/2" wide. (Collector tip: Made by Griffen, Smith and Hill of Phoenixville, Pa., 1879 to about 1890.)

$500+

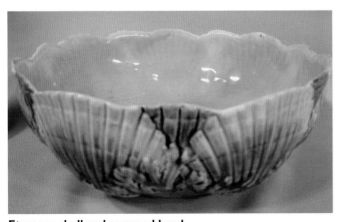

Etruscan shell and seaweed bowl
8 1/2", rim nicks, hairline crack, good color.

$200+

Etruscan shell and seaweed bowl
rim wear, 8 1/2" diameter.

$125+

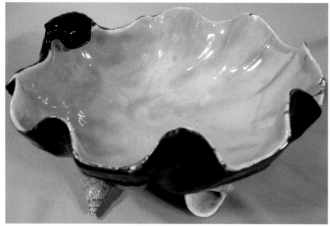

Holdcroft cobalt shell bowl
with three shell feet, 9 1/2" diameter. (Collector tip: Joseph Holdcroft majolica ware was produced at Daisy Bank in Longton, Staffordshire, England, from 1870 to 1885. Items can be found marked with "JHOLDCROFT," but many items can only be attributed by the patterns and colors that are documented to have come from the Holdcroft potteries.)

$275+

Holdcroft footed bowl
large pond lily, 11" diameter.

$200+

Hugo Lonitz figural
Blackamoor center bowl, rim repair to bowl, 11" long, 8" tall. (Collector tip: Hugo Lonitz operated in Haldensleben, Germany, from 1868-1886, and later Hugo Lonitz & Co., 1886-1904, producing household and decorative porcelain and earthenware, and metal wares. Look for a mark of two entwined fish.)

$400+

Six grape leaf bowls
various sizes and conditions.

$275+ all

Six grape leaf bowls
various conditions.

$250+ all

Seven grape-leaf bowls
various sizes and conditions.

$250+ all

Wedgwood Argenta
angel and putti center bowl and tray, hairline crack to bowl. (Collector tip:
Founded by Josiah Wedgwood in 1759 at Burslem, Staffordshire, England.)

$225+

Busts and Figures

Majolica bust and figurines are highly prized, but also present some special challenges for collectors. The fine details that are so admired can hide significant restoration, so extra care must be taken to get a solid provenance, which would include details about repairs and color touch-ups.

Pair of Blackamoors
reclining boy with melon and girl, each 6" long.

$225+ pair

Pair of French busts
of man and woman, each 18" tall, various nicks and repairs.

$275+ pair

Pair of Blackamoor figures
terra-cotta, lady with baskets of flowers and umbrella, man with suitcase, umbrella and top hat, good detail, minor nicks, each 14" tall.

$200+ pair

Continental cats
under tree figure, unusual, 5 3/4" tall.

$50+

Figure of boy
on pillow balancing covered egg with feet, professional repair
to cover, 8 1/2" tall.

$10+

Figures of man and woman
each with basket of flowers, good detail, each 14" tall.

$100+ pair

Three Jerome Massier singing frogs
two with song books and one with mandolin, repair to foot of one with mandolin and chip to another foot of one with the song book, 3 1/4" to 4 1/2" tall. (Collector tip: The Massier family began
producing ceramics in Vallauris, France, in the mid-18th century.)

$1,200 all

Minton Hogarth girl

with basket figural, hairline crack to basket, 7 1/2" tall. (William Hogarth [1697–1764], English painter and engraver, humorist and satirist.)

$350+

Minton pedestal

with figures of young hunters with dog and game, shape no. 657, date code for 1866, 8 1/2" tall. (Thomas Minton founded his factory in the mid-1790s in Stoke-on-Trent, Staffordshire, England. His son, Herbert Minton, introduced majolica pottery—with glazes created by Léon Arnoux—at England's Great Exhibition of 1851.)

$175+

Minton parrot

on stump figure, 12 1/2" tall.

$700+

Minton putti shell carriers

on cobalt rimmed base, strong color and detail, 11" wide, 11" tall.

$3,000+

Minton "vintager" boy
(a person who harvests grapes) with basket, professional base and jacket repair, 8" tall. (Thomas Minton founded his factory in the mid-1790s in Stoke-on-Trent, Staffordshire, England. His son, Herbert Minton, introduced majolica pottery—with glazes created by Léon Arnoux—at England's Great Exhibition of 1851.)

$200+

Minton "vintager" boy
with basket, loss of thumb, repair to coattail, 7 1/2" tall.

$800+

Wedgwood figure
of lady gathering wheat in field, minor hairline crack, great detail, rare figural, 20 1/2" tall. (Collector tip: Founded by Josiah Wedgwood in 1759 at Burslem, Staffordshire, England.)

$2,500+

Wedgwood figure
of lady with jug of water at spring, great detail, rare figural, 21" tall.

$2,500+

Butter Pats

Some majolica pieces listed here are valued in groups, and are representative of what a collector might find at large auction or private sale. Some pieces are grouped by color or style, others by use, and a few by manufacturer. The phrase "various conditions" is shorthand for a range of cracks, chips, flaking, repairs, crazing and staining. Rare or important pieces of majolica will usually have a provenance, and any repairs or restorations should be noted when they are sold.

Though assortments may offer limited information on the value of any single piece, they are an excellent place for beginning collectors to start gathering information on makers, marks, years of production and rarity.

Four begonia leaf
on basket butter pats.

$275+ all

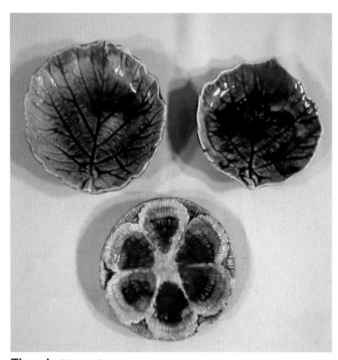

Three butter pats
various conditions.

$80+ all

Four butter pats
various conditions.

$100+ all

Five butter pats
various conditions.

$120+ all

Copeland pansy
butter pat, good color.

$125+

Copeland pansy
butter pat, good color, minor glaze miss on rim.

$200+

Copeland pansy
butter pat, good color.

$150+

Etruscan begonia leaf
on basket butter pat. (Collector tip: Made by Griffen, Smith and Hill of Phoenixville, Pa., 1879 to about 1890.)

$60+

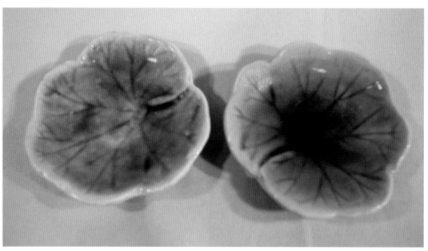

Pair of Etruscan geranium
butter pats.

$60+ pair

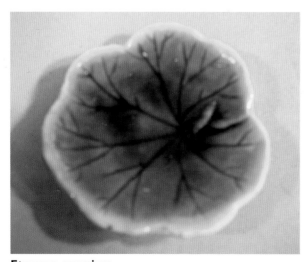

Etruscan geranium
butter pat.

$25+

Etruscan green pond lily
butter pat.

$25+

Four Etruscan maple leaf
on plate butter pats, one with minor rim nick. (Collector tip: Made by Griffen, Smith and Hill of Phoenixville, Pa., 1879 to about 1890.)

$225+ all

Etruscan multi-color pansy
butter pat.

$30+

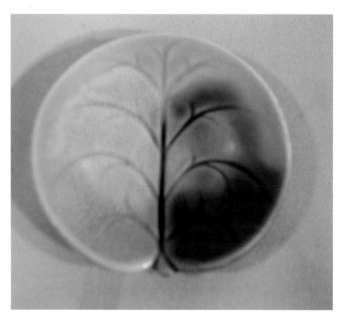

Etruscan pond lily
butter pat.

$110+

Eureka fan-shaped
butter pat with pink ground, minor rim glaze nick. (Collector tip: Eureka Pottery of Trenton, N.J., circa 1883-1887.)

$130+

Fielding butter pat
with Oriental ship and fan motif, rim nick, rare. (Collector tip: Railway Pottery, established by S. Fielding & Co., Stoke, Stoke-on-Trent, Staffordshire, England, 1879.)

$275+

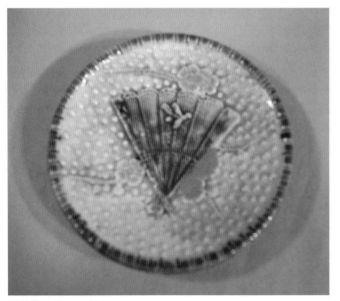

Fielding fan and insect
butter pat with light green ground, hairline crack.

$110+

Fielding fan and insect
butter pat with white ground.

$150+

Fish-shaped butter pat
rare, 4 3/4" long.

$400+

Maple leaf on basket
butter pat, minor rim wear.

$30+

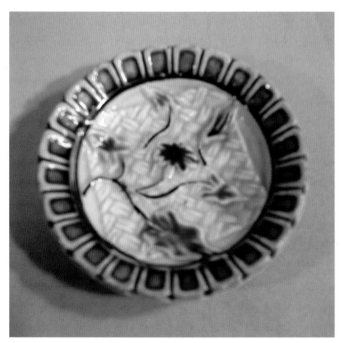

Morning glory on napkin
butter pat.

$200+

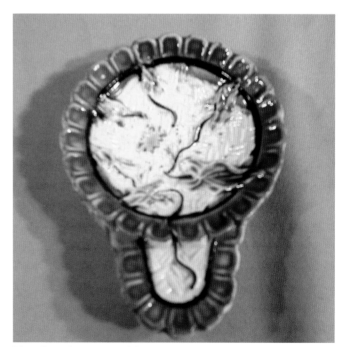

Morning glory on napkin
butter pat with handle, rim and surface wear.

$50+

Mottled leaf
butter pat and multicolored leaf butter pat.

$40+ pair

Mottled leaf
butter pat.

$30+

Mottled pink
green, yellow and brown butter pat.

$10+

Shell and seaweed
butter pat.

$30+

Cachepots

A term seldom heard today, a cachepot is an ornamental casing for a flowerpot, of ceramic materials, or metal, paper, etc.

Also see jardinières.

Holdcroft pond lily foot cachepot
strong color and detail, 7" diameter, 5 3/4" tall, $700+ (Collector tip: Joseph Holdcroft majolica ware was produced at Daisy Bank in Longton, Staffordshire, England, from 1870 to 1885. Items can be found marked with "JHOLDCROFT," but many items can only be attributed by the patterns and colors that are documented to have come from the Holdcroft potteries.)

$700+

Bamboo, ribbon and bow cachepot
with under plate, minor rim nick to cachepot, rim chips to tray, 7 1/2" tall, 8" diameter.

$375+

George Jones picket fence
and floral cachepot with stand, hairline crack to pot and stand, 8" tall, 8" diameter. (Collector tip: The company started operations in the early 1860s as George Jones in Stoke, Staffordshire, England, and in 1873 became George Jones & Sons Ltd.)

$300+

George Jones picket fence
and floral cachepot with stand, rim wear to pot, 8" tall, 8" diameter.

$400+

George Jones
diamond-shaped cachepot, cobalt ground with bamboo borders, storks, water lilies and flowers in relief, outstanding color and detail, 11 1/2" long, 7" tall.

$5,750+

Leaves and fern cachepot
5 1/2" tall.

$120+

Rorstrand cachepot
8" tall, 8 3/4" diameter, hairline, rim and base chip. (Collector tip: The Rörstrand factory made the first faience (tin-glazed earthenware) produced in Sweden. It was established in 1725 by Johann Wolff, near Stockholm.)

$25+

Cake Stands

If the idea of a special stand for displaying and serving cakes seems old fashioned, well, it is, but that was the mindset of the Victorian age: everything at the table had a unique use that, when taken together, created the perfect and complete dining experience. Cake stands came in several heights, and the taller examples tend to show more wear or damage simply because they were not as steady during the cake cutting.

Bird on branch
low cake stand, 8 3/4" diameter.

$60+

Cake stand
with fans and butterflies, 8 3/4" diameter, 2 3/4" tall.

$325
Courtesy of Joan Sween

Etruscan conventional cake stand
hard to find, strong color, 10" diameter, 4 3/4" tall. (Collector tip: Made by Griffen, Smith and Hill of Phoenixville, Pa., 1879 to about 1890.)

$375+

Etruscan maple leaves
cake stand.

$150+

Etruscan maple leaves
cake stand.

$150+

Etruscan pink maple leaves
cake stand, great color, 9 1/4" diameter, 5 1/4" tall.

$225+

Pond lily and stork
tall cake stand, good detail, 9 1/2" tall, 10 1/2" diameter.

$400+

Wedgwood tall dolphin
footed cake stand with scenic center, 9" diameter, 5" tall. (Collector tip: Founded by Josiah Wedgwood in 1759 at Burslem, Staffordshire, England.)

$400+

Candleholder

Unlike the 20th century accessories that usually were part of a console set, many vintage majolica candleholders often were sold and used individually and as pairs.

Pair of Hooligans
at lamppost figural candleholders, each 6 3/4" tall, one with chips and head reattached.

$65+ pair

Pair of George Jones
putti candleholders/bases, repair to one arm, loss of fingers, early staple repair to base of one, each 12 1/4" tall. (Collector tip: The company started operations in the early 1860s as George Jones in Stoke, Staffordshire, England, and in 1873 became George Jones & Sons Ltd.)

$500+ pair

Minton dolphin candlestick
professional repair to top, 8 1/4" tall. (Thomas Minton founded his factory in the mid-1790s in Stoke-on-Trent, Staffordshire, England. His son, Herbert Minton, introduced majolica pottery—with glazes created by Léon Arnoux—at England's Great Exhibition of 1851.)

$450+

Centerpiece

The wonderful thing about majolica centerpieces is that they offer no excuses for their existence: they have no purpose other than to look whimsical, or stunning, or garish, depending on your point of view and the imagination of the designer.

French triple-swan
table centerpiece, good detail, professional repair to wings and tail of one swan, 16 1/4" diameter, 8" tall.

$800

Gerbing & Stephen
(Czechoslovakia) crescent-shaped pierced centerpiece, 1880s, 9" tall.

$250
Courtesy of Joan Sween

George Jones
table centerpiece with putto riding dolphin atop shell and coral base while holding shell, rim chip to one shell and hairline to another, outstanding color and detail, 15" tall, 13 1/2" wide. (Collector tip: The company started operations in the early 1860s as George Jones in Stoke, Staffordshire, England, and in 1873 became George Jones & Sons Ltd.)

$3,500+

George Jones water lily
and basket-weave round table centerpiece flower holder, outstanding color and detail, minor hairline, 15" diameter, 2" tall.

$4,250+

Minton lovebirds
and putti table centerpiece, losses to laurel drape and arms, hairline to top, 10 3/4" long, 6 3/4" tall.

$1200-$1500

Minton mermaids
and shell table centerpiece with laurel garlands, date code for 1866, minor hairline to laurel garland, great detail and color, 17 1/2" long, 10" tall. (Thomas Minton founded his factory in the mid-1790s in Stoke-on-Trent, Staffordshire, England. His son, Herbert Minton, introduced majolica pottery—with glazes created by Léon Arnoux—at England's Great Exhibition of 1851.)

$9,500+

Minton rabbits
under cabbage table centerpiece, shape no. 1451, date code for 1873, strong color and detail, 9 1/2" long, 4 1/2" tall.

$7500-$10,000

Wedgwood nautilus centerpiece
with double dolphin supports, also marked with impressed "GA," circa 1880, 16 3/8" tall. (Collector tip: Founded by Josiah Wedgwood in 1759 at Burslem, Staffordshire, England.)

$1,800
Courtesy of Joan Sween

Minton turquoise
nautilus shell centerpiece supported by two mermen, shell has putti in high relief and a maiden atop shell, outstanding color and detail, minor repair to foot of maiden, shape no. 992, date code for 1874, 20 1/2" tall, 17 1/2" wide.

$10,000+

Cheese Keepers

Like oyster plates, tableware related to serving cheese has become a popular collecting area in itself. Dome-shaped pieces are sometimes called "cheese bells."

Bird on branch
cheese keeper with ribbon and bow accents, professional rim repair to base and cover, 7" tall.

$400+

Cobalt cheese keeper
with cow on one side and bull on the other among apple trees with apple finial, strong color and detail, minor nicks to cover base rim, attributed to Forester, 11" tall.

$1,500+

Cobalt bird on branch
and water lily cheese keeper, good color, hairline crack and base chip to cover, 7" tall.

$550+

George Jones apple blossom
full-size cheese keeper, strong color, hairline to cover, 12 1/2" tall. (Collector tip: The company started operations in the early 1860s as George Jones in Stoke, Staffordshire, England, and in 1873 became George Jones & Sons Ltd.)

$2,500+

George Jones cobalt
picket fence and daisy full-size cheese keeper, outstanding color, minor professional rim repair to under plate, 12" diameter, 12" tall.

$10,000+

George Jones picket fence
and floral cheese keeper, full size, professional hairline repair and handle repair to cover, 11" tall.

$6-$8,000

George Jones turquoise
apple blossom and basket-weave cheese keeper, strong color, minor hairline to cover, 10" tall.

$2,000+

George Jones turquoise
daisy floral cheese keeper, good color, professional rim repair to base, 10 1/2" diameter, 7 1/2" tall.

$3,500+

Mottled wedge cheese keeper
9 3/4" long, 6" tall.

$125+

Pink rope and fern
paneled cheese keeper, hairline crack and rim chip to base, 11" diameter, 10" tall.

$650+

Wedge-shaped orchid
cheese keeper, good detail, professional repair to corner of base, Bacall Collection, 12" long, 8" tall.

$450+

Comports (compotes)

Some majolica pieces listed here are valued in groups, and are representative of what a collector might find at large auction or private sale. Some pieces are grouped by color or style, others by use, and a few by manufacturer. The phrase "various conditions" is shorthand for a range of cracks, chips, flaking, repairs, crazing and staining. Rare or important pieces of majolica will usually have a provenance, and any repairs or restorations should be noted when they are sold.

Though assortments may offer limited information on the value of any single piece, they are an excellent place for beginning collectors to start gathering information on makers, marks, years of production and rarity.

Begonia leaf
and basket-weave deep comport (or compote) and sunflower comport, various conditions.

$125+ pair

Bellflower compote
probably English, 9 1/2" diameter, 5 1/4" tall.

$285
Courtesy of Joan Sween

Brownfield strawberry comport
(compote), great color and detail, 9 1/2" long. (Collector tip: W. Brownfield & Son, Burslem and Cobridge, Staffordshire, England, 1850 to 1891.)

$175+

Cobalt bell flower
and begonia leaf comport (compote), outstanding color, 9 1/2" diameter, 5 1/4" tall.

$275+

Continental comport
(compote) with reticulated rim, leaves, ferns and floral motif, 9" diameter, 4 1/4" tall.

$65+

Etruscan albino shell
and seaweed comport (compote), minor hairline crack. (Collector tip: Made by Griffen, Smith and Hill of Phoenixville, Pa., 1879 to about 1890.)

$250+

Etruscan cobalt daisy comport
(compote), minor hairline crack and rim nick, 9" diameter, 5" tall.

$150+

Etruscan cobalt daisy comport
(compote), 8 3/4" diameter.

$225+

Etruscan cobalt daisy comport
(compote), 8 1/2" diameter.

$250+

Etruscan maple leaf
shallow compote, with early mark for Griffen, Smith and Hill, 9" diameter, 5 1/2" tall.

$250
Courtesy of Joan Sween

Fielding fishnet
and shell comport (compote) and turquoise wild rose and rope comport, various conditions.

$250+ pair

Gerbing & Stephen
(Czechoslovakia) figural comport (compote), various repairs, 16" tall, 15 1/2" wide.

$55+

Holdcroft cobalt leaf comport
(compote), strong color, hairline crack, 9 1/4" diameter. (Collector tip: Joseph Holdcroft majolica ware was produced at Daisy Bank in Longton, Staffordshire, England, from 1870 to 1885. Items can be found marked with "JHOLDCROFT," but many items can only be attributed by the patterns and colors that are documented to have come from the Holdcroft potteries.)

$175+

Large French figural comport
(compote) with mermen and seahorses supporting bowl with mythological faces, minor professional repairs to feet of seahorse and rim of bowl, great detail, attributed to Thomas Sergeant, 15 1/2" tall.

$1,500

Pair of Holdcroft
pond lily comports (compotes), both with rim chips.

$200+ pair

Holdcroft mottled shell comport
(or compote) with shells and seaweed on base, good detail, 9 1/2" diameter, 7" tall.

$325+

Holdcroft pond lily
low comport (compote), 8 3/4" diameter.

$225+

George Jones chestnut leaf
on napkin low comport (compote), 9 1/4" diameter. (Collector tip: The company started operations in the early 1860s as George Jones in Stoke, Staffordshire, England, and in 1873 became George Jones & Sons Ltd.)

$200+

George Jones chestnut leaf
on napkin low comport (or compote), 9 1/4" diameter.

$200+

George Jones pond lily comport
(compote) with water lily, cattail and lily pad base, great detail, repair to base, hairline crack to top, 9 1/2" diameter, 5 1/2" tall.

$1,200

George Jones turquoise shell comport
(compote), professional rim repair, 9" diameter, 5" tall.

$250+

Samuel Lear classical urn

and sunflower comport (or compote) with lavender rim, 9" diameter, 3" tall. (Collector tip: Samuel Lear, Hanley, Staffordshire, England, 1877 to 1886.)

$180+

Maple leaf and basket comport

(compote) with pink trim, good color, 9" diameter, 5" tall.

$225+

Morley & Co.

mottled leaf comport (or compote), rim repair. (Morley & Co. Pottery was founded in 1879, Wellsville, Ohio, making graniteware and majolica.)

$110+

Turquoise and cobalt

cauliflower comport (or compote), good color, 9 3/4" diameter, 5" tall.

$250+

Wedgwood Argenta

strawberry comport (or compote), 8 1/2" diameter. (Collector tip: Founded by Josiah Wedgwood in 1759 at Burslem, Staffordshire, England.)

$120+

Wedgwood Classical-style
lion footed comport (compote) with floral reticulated top, strong color and detail, professional repair to base, 9" diameter, 5 1/2" tall.

$175+

Wedgwood Classical-style
lion footed comport (compote) with water lily and dragonfly reticulated top, great color and detail, professional rim repair, 9" diameter, 5 1/2" tall.

$300+

Wedgwood maple leaf
and floral compote, strong color, also marked, "9V29 Made in England," 11 1/4" wide, 5 3/8" tall.

$290
Courtesy of Joan Sween

Pair of Wedgwood
triple dolphin and shell comports (compotes), repair to pedestals, hairline crack, rim nicks, 9" diameter, 7" tall.

$400+ pair

Creamers and Sugars

Some majolica pieces listed here are valued in groups, and are representative of what a collector might find at large auction or private sale. Some pieces are grouped by color or style, others by use, and a few by manufacturer. The phrase "various conditions" is shorthand for a range of cracks, chips, flaking, repairs, crazing and staining. Rare or important pieces of majolica will usually have a provenance, and any repairs or restorations should be noted when they are sold.

Though assortments may offer limited information on the value of any single piece, they are an excellent place for beginning collectors to start gathering information on makers, marks, years of production and rarity.

Nine creamers
and one sugar, various conditions.

$300+ all

Basket-weave
and rose flat creamer.

$100+

Etruscan corn
creamer, 4" tall.

$110+

Floral covered sugar

$110+

Holdcroft figural

coconut creamer with Chinaman handle, matches Holdcroft Chinaman and coconut teapot, extremely rare, 5" long, 2 1/2" tall. (Collector tip: Joseph Holdcroft majolica ware was produced at Daisy Bank in Longton, Staffordshire, England, from 1870 to 1885. Items can be found marked with "JHOLDCROFT," but many items can only be attributed by the patterns and colors that are documented to have come from the Holdcroft potteries.)

$500+

Holdcroft mottled

honeycomb creamer, minor hairline crack.

$60+

Holdcroft pond lily

creamer, minor rim nick.

$35+

George Jones rustic
floral creamer, Bacall Collection, 3" tall. (Collector tip: The company started operations in the early 1860s as George Jones in Stoke, Staffordshire, England, and in 1873 became George Jones & Sons Ltd.)
$350+

George Jones turquoise
strawberry leaf creamer, 3 1/2" tall.
$325+

Samuel Lear water lily
creamer and sugar, handle repair to sugar. (Collector tip: Samuel Lear, Hanley, Staffordshire, England, 1877 to 1886.)
$50+ pair

Samuel Lear water lily
creamer and sugar, hairline crack to creamer, nicks to sugar lid.

$110+ pair

Pineapple creamer
minor spout nick, 3 3/4" tall.

$90+

Pineapple creamer
2 3/4" tall.

$70+

Turquoise floral
creamer and sugar, minor nick to creamer.

$85+ pair

Wardle bamboo
and fern creamer, nick to spout and handle, 4 1/4" tall. (Collector tip: Wardle & Co., established 1871 at Hanley, Staffordshire, England.)

$40+

Wardle floral
and leaf covered sugar, 5" tall.

$130+

Fourteen assorted creamers
various conditions.

$375+ all

Cups and Saucers

Along with pitchers and teapots, majolica cups and saucers are the most prone to damage. Collectors should check for handle repairs and wear to rims. And remember: Because of the lead- and tin-based glazes used in vintage majolica, these pieces should never be used for food and beverage serving or storage.

Blackberry and basket-weave
cup and saucer, good color, hairline to cup.

$120+ pair

Pair of cobalt cranes
in flight and water lily cups and saucers, good color, hairline crack to cups.

$225+ all

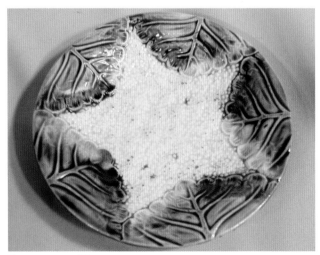

Etruscan cauliflower saucer
strong color.

$75+

Etruscan shell
and seaweed cup and saucer.

$125+ pair

Pair of Etruscan

shell and seaweed cups and saucers, minor rim nick to one cup.

$325+ all

Three sets of Etruscan

shell and seaweed cups and saucers.

$350+ all

Fielding bird and fan

turquoise cup and saucer. (Collector tip: Railway Pottery, established by S. Fielding & Co., Stoke, Stoke-on-Trent, Staffordshire, England, 1879.)

$125+ pair

George Jones turquoise

basket-weave and floral saucer, good color, 5 1/2" diameter.

$400+

Holdcroft honeycomb

cup and saucer. (Collector tip: Joseph Holdcroft majolica ware was produced at Daisy Bank in Longton, Staffordshire, England, from 1870 to 1885. Items can be found marked with "JHOLDCROFT," but many items can only be attributed by the patterns and colors that are documented to have come from the Holdcroft potteries.)

$200+ pair

Pineapple
cup and saucer, minor nick to saucer.

$125+ pair

Shorter and Bolton
three sets of bird and fan cups and saucers, hairline to one cup.

$250+ all

Wardle bamboo and fern
cup and saucer. (Collector tip: Wardle & Co., established 1871 at Hanley, Staffordshire, England.)

$125+ pair

Wedgwood cauliflower
cup and saucer, good color. (Collector tip: Founded by Josiah Wedgwood in 1759 at Burslem, Staffordshire, England.)

$100+ pair

Dishes (Assorted)

Some majolica pieces listed here are valued in groups, and are representative of what a collector might find at large auction or private sale. Some pieces are grouped by color or style, others by use, and a few by manufacturer. The phrase "various conditions" is shorthand for a range of cracks, chips, flaking, repairs, crazing and staining. Rare or important pieces of majolica will usually have a provenance, and any repairs or restorations should be noted when they are sold.

Though assortments may offer limited information on the value of any single piece, they are an excellent place for beginning collectors to start gathering information on makers, marks, years of production and rarity.

Also see plates, platters, trays and sauce dishes.

Samuel Alcock butter dish
three pieces, with shrimp handle atop bed of leaves, ferns and flowers, 6 1/2" diameter. (Collector tip: Another Staffordshire potter, Samuel Alcock & Co., Cobridge, 1828-53; Burslem, 1830-59, produced earthenware, china, parian.)
$900+

Seven begonia leaf dishes
various conditions.

$400+ all

Dishes (Assorted)

Seven begonia leaf dishes
various conditions.

$325+ all

Seven begonia leaf dishes
various conditions.

$375+ all

Four unusual bone dishes

$40+ all

Four Etruscan
begonia leaf dishes various conditions. (Collector tip: Made by Griffen, Smith and Hill of Phoenixville, Pa., 1879 to about 1890.)

$275+ all

Four Etruscan
begonia leaf dishes various conditions.

$300+ all

Six Etruscan
begonia leaf dishes, various conditions.

$350+ all

Four Etruscan
begonia leaf dishes, various conditions.

$275+ all

Etruscan daisy
pickle dish, hairline crack, 6 1/2" wide.

$200+

Pair of Etruscan
leaf dishes, minor nicks.

$175+ pair

George Jones
quail game dish, great color, 11 3/4" long. (Collector tip: The company started operations in the early 1860s as George Jones in Stoke, Staffordshire, England, and in 1873 became George Jones & Sons Ltd.)

$600+

Victoria Pottery Co.
(VPC) basket-weave game dish with mallard ducks on bed of ferns on cover, good color, with insert, professional repair to duck's wing, 12" wide. (Collector tip: Victoria Pottery Co., Hanley, Staffordshire, England, 1895 to 1927.)

$600+

Wardle bird and fan
covered butter dish, hairline crack to base, 8 1/2" diameter. (Collector tip: Wardle & Co., established 1871 at Hanley, Staffordshire, England.)

$150+

Wedgwood lovebirds
game dish with winged gryphon handles, flowers, leaves, game, ribbon and bows in relief, rim chip to bottom of cover, 10" wide. (Collector tip: Founded by Josiah Wedgwood in 1759 at Burslem, Staffordshire, England.)

$600+

Eggcups and Holders

Like oyster plates, tableware related to serving eggs has become a popular collecting area in itself.

Basket-weave and ivy
eggcup holder and four eggcups, repair to handle and two eggcups.

$60+ all

Julius Dressler leaf tray
with six eggcups, 13" wide. (Collector tip: Julius Dressler, Bela Czech Republic, company founded 1888, producing faience, majolica and porcelain. In 1920, the name was changed to EPIAG. The firm closed about 1945.)

$70+ all

Floral
double eggcup holder with eggcups, rim chip to one eggcup and to holder.

$250+

Turquoise and pink
basket-weave egg holder basket, 7 1/4" diameter.

$170+

Ewers

Also see jugs and pitchers.

Brownfield ewer
with putti, leaves and flowers in high relief and putti handle, professional rim and base repair, 16 1/2" tall. (Collector tip: W. Brownfield & Son, Burslem and Cobridge, Staffordshire, England, 1850-1891.)

$1,200-$1,500

Pair of Brownfield
ram's head ewers with ribbon and drapes of leaves and roses in high relief, professional handle, base and rim repairs, each 14" tall.

$200+ pair

Copeland ewer
with angel faces and birds in high relief, band of ivy and berries on cobalt ground, good color, professional spout and handle repair, 10 1/2" tall. (Collector tip: William T. Copeland & Sons pottery of Stoke-on-Trent, England, began producing porcelain and earthenware in 1847.)

$1,200

Hugo Lonitz
cobalt ewer with swan atop cattails, strong color and detail, professional repair to handle, 15" tall. (Collector tip: Hugo Lonitz operated in Haldensleben, Germany, from 1868-1886, and later Hugo Lonitz & Co., 1886-1904, producing household and decorative porcelain and earthenware, and metal wares. Look for a mark of two entwined fish.)

$1,200+

French Minton
miniature lemon ewer and orange ewer, repairs.

$50+ pair

Humidors

In the Victorian era, pipe smokers often kept their tobacco in a decorative tobacco jar or humidor. Figural tobacco jars were mainly ceramic, typically heads or full figures of people and animals. Manufacturers in Austria and Germany turned out millions of humidors in the middle to late Victorian era, when pipe smoking replaced snuff as the preferred means of using tobacco. Collector tip: Contemporary figural humidors are usually lighter in weight than vintage examples, but designs and glazes may make them look older than they really are.

Baby girl
with bonnet humidor, 5" tall.

$80+

Bird and fan
turquoise humidor, 5 1/2" tall.

$150+

Continental figural
tiger head humidor, base repaired, nick to lid, 4" tall.

$50+

Duck with red cape
humidor, 5 1/2" tall.

$250+

Figural elephant
with red smoking jacket humidor, minor rim nick to lid, 7" tall.

$250+

Figural face humidor
of train engineer with cap, nick to cap, 6" tall.

$80+

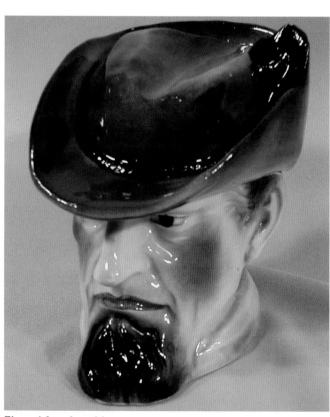

Figural face humidor
of man with goatee, age unknown, 5" tall.

$40+

Figural lady duck
with bonnet humidor, unusual form, 8 3/4" tall.

$450+

Figural pig
newlyweds humidor, chip to lid, Portugal, age unknown, 8" tall.

$100+

Fisherman
with beard and pipe humidor, 6" tall.

$70+

German fox
humidor, 4 3/4" tall.

$200+

Girl with long hair
and red headscarf humidor, 5" tall.

$60+

Indian head humidor
7" tall, age unknown.

$10+

Indian maiden face humidor
good detail, rim nicks to lid, 5 1/2" tall.

$60+

Large Indian chief humidor
minor nick to feather, age unknown, 7 3/4" tall.

$25+

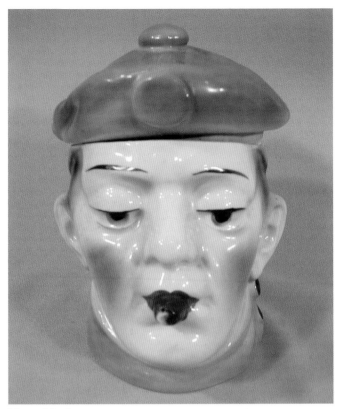

Man with cigar
face humidor, hairline crack, age unknown, 5 1/2" tall.

$10+

Man with green hat
humidor, age unknown, 7" tall.

$25+

Oriental lady
humidor, 5" tall.

$40+

Portugal pig
with apron and broom figural humidor, age unknown, 8" tall.

$175+

Inkwells

Majolica inkwells range from simple floral forms to the wildly unexpected, including the two examples here, which show cats and an alligator riding bicycles. Both of these have had professional repairs, which hold their values down.

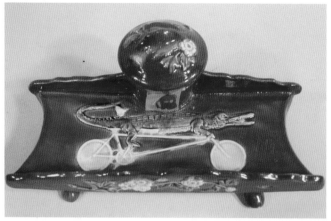

Continental inkwell
with alligator riding bicycle, professional repairs to lid and to rim and feet of base, 8 1/2" long.

$50+

Continental inkwell
with cats on bicycles and floral design, professional leg and rim repair to base, 8 1/2" long.

$75+

Continental figural
frog inkwell with glass insert, minor nicks to tips of flowers, 3 1/4" tall.

$700+

French figural
horse inkwell, very unusual, ears professionally restored, 10 1/2" wide.

$400+

Jardinières

In the early 20th century, American makers like Roseville produced dozens of styles of jardinières in "blended" glazes that echoed the majolica wares of 50 years earlier, and these can still be purchased for a fraction of the values found on period pieces.

Monumental Copeland
floor jardinière with large vine handles and rim of grape clusters, great cobalt ground with faces of mythological figures in high relief, good color and detail, professional repair to one handle, 29" wide, 17" tall. (Collector tip: William T. Copeland & Sons pottery of Stoke-on-Trent, England, began producing porcelain and earthenware in 1847.)

$3,250+

French jardinière
with applied flowers on painted ground, good detail, nicks to flowers, 8" diameter, 7 1/2" tall.

$100+

Large French birds
on branch, blackberry, floral and leaves oval jardinière, good detail, 15" wide, 8" tall.

$500+

Thomas Forester cobalt
bird, water lily and cattail footed oval window jardinière, outstanding color and detail, 17 1/2" long, 7 1/2" tall. (Collector tip: There were two Thomas Forester potteries active in the late 19th century in Staffordshire, England. Some sources list the more famous of the two as Thomas Forester & Sons Ltd. at the Phoenix works, Longton.)

$1,000+

Holdcroft pond lily
oval window jardinière, very unusual form, strong color and detail, footed, minor professional rim repair, 17" long, 6 1/2" tall.

$1,400+

Holdcroft cobalt
footed jardinière with ladies head handles and garland drapes, good color, professional rim repair, 11" wide, 7" tall. (Collector tip: Joseph Holdcroft majolica ware was produced at Daisy Bank in Longton, Staffordshire, England, from 1870 to 1885. Items can be found marked with "JHOLDCROFT," but many items can only be attributed by the patterns and colors that are documented to have come from the Holdcroft potteries.)

$400+

Holdcroft turquoise
floral jardinière and under plate, cobalt accent, strong color and detail, professional base and rim repair, 9" tall, 9" diameter.

$300+

George Jones cobalt
jardinière stand with leaf motif, 8" diameter. (Collector tip: The company started operations in the early 1860s as George Jones in Stoke, Staffordshire, England, and in 1873 became George Jones & Sons Ltd.)

$275+

George Jones cobalt
water lily and fly jardinière with bamboo base, professional rim and base repair, strong color, 10" wide, 8 1/2" tall.

$800+

George Jones
crate and insect footed jardinière, unusual form, good color, old staple repair, chip, 7 3/4" tall, 7" wide.

$125+

Minton cobalt
"Asia/Europe" pedestal cachepot/jardinière, strong color and detail, shape no. 1389, date code for 1869, professional rim repair, 13 1/2" tall, 12" wide. (Thomas Minton founded his factory in the mid-1790s in Stoke-on-Trent, Staffordshire, England. His son, Herbert Minton, introduced majolica pottery—with glazes created by Léon Arnoux—at England's Great Exhibition of 1851.)

$4-$6,000

Minton ram's head jardinière
professional repair to rams heads, rim and base, good color, 14 3/4" tall, 19 1/2" wide.

$1,500

Mottled jardinière
with angel faces around rim, 9" tall, 10" diameter.

$80+

Thomas Sergent Palissy
shells, fern and leaf jardinière, great detail, 7 1/2" tall, 10" diameter. (Collector tip: Thomas-Victor Sergent was one of the School of Paris ceramists of the late 19th century who was influenced by the works of Bernard Palissy, c. 1510-1590, the great French Renaissance potter.)

$800+

Jugs

Also see ewers and pitchers.

Continental figural
melon jug, 11 1/2" tall.

$25+

Field jug
French, 10" tall, unmarked.

$550+
Courtesy the Iridescent House

Minton tower jug
with jester finial on hinged silver lid, shape no. 1231, professional repair to thumb lift on cover, 13" tall. (Thomas Minton founded his factory in the mid-1790s in Stoke-on-Trent, Staffordshire, England. His son, Herbert Minton, introduced majolica pottery with glazes created by Léon Arnoux—at England's Great Exhibition of 1851.)

$750+

Minton tower jug
with jester finial on hinged pewter lid, shape no. 1231, 13" tall.

$850+

Nimy "Dranem"
full-figure Toby jug, rare, 13" tall. (Collector tip: Nimy-lez-Mons, Belgium.)

$350+

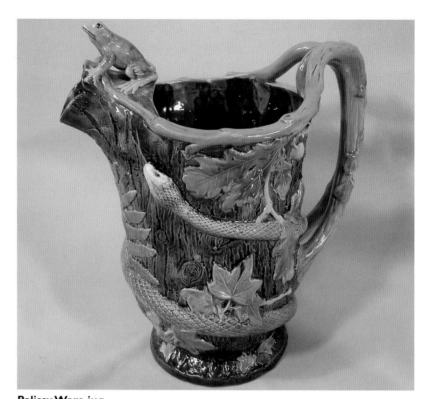

Palissy Ware jug
with oak leaves, acorns and snake wrapped around jug with frog on spout, professional rim, handle and spout repair, 10" tall. (Collector tip: In the style of Bernard Palissy, c. 1510-1590, the great French Renaissance potter.)

$1,100+

Sarreguemines double-face jug
#2313, professional rim repair, 8 1/2" tall. (Collector tip: Named for the city in the Alsace-Lorraine region of northeastern France.)

$150+

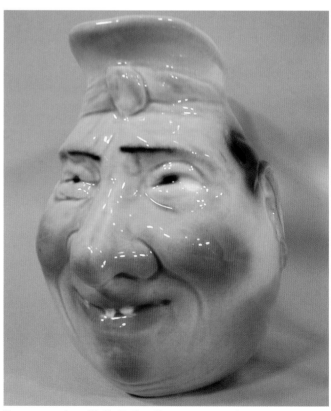

Sarreguemines "Jolly Fellow"
#3181 face jug, 8 1/2" tall.

$125+

Sarreguemines "Jolly Fellow"
#3181 face jug, 5 1/2" tall.

$90+

Sarreguemines "Jolly Fellow"
#3181 face jug, 6" tall.

$100+

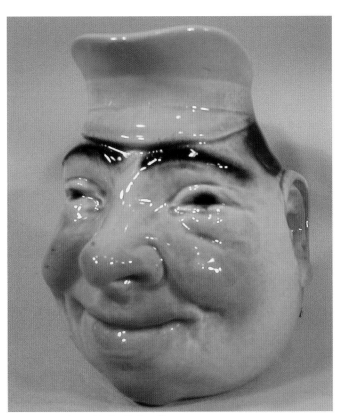

Sarreguemines "Jolly Fellow"
#3181 face jug, 5 1/2" tall.

$100+

Sarreguemines "The English"
#3210 face jug, solid green, 8" tall.

$125+

Sarreguemines "The English"
#3210 face jug, 8" tall.

$125+

Sarreguemines face jug
#3611, 8 1/2" tall.

$200+

Sarreguemines-type face jug
No. 7889, "The Scotsman," 8 3/4" tall, rim repair.

$150+

Sarreguemines-type face jug
#7890 "Green Hat with Pink Bow," 8 3/4" tall.

$350+

Sarreguemines-type face jug
#7892, "Matelot," 8 1/2" tall.

$150+

Sarreguemines-type face jug
#8715, "Frowning Face," 7" tall. (Collector tip: Named for the city in the Alsace-Lorraine region of northeastern France.)

$350+

Sarreguemines-type face jug
with removable lid and matte-finish face, 9 1/2" tall.

$400+

Wedgwood 1876 Centennial jug
with bust of Washington and Lincoln on each side, cobalt accent, minor rim glaze nick, 5 1/2" tall. (Collector tip: Founded by Josiah Wedgwood in 1759 at Burslem, Staffordshire, England.)

$575+

Match Boxes and Strikers

It is rare to find a figural match striker that has not had some wear and tear over the years, so look closely for signs of repair.

"BB" figural match striker
with mouse, melon, flowers and leaves, minor rim repair, 8" wide.

$550+

"B Block" figural Blackamoor
with baskets match striker, outstanding color and detail, minor repair to rim of basket, head reattached, 10 1/2" tall.

$350+

Blackamoor lady
with vases match striker, 8 1/2" tall.

$225+

Blackamoor man
riding elephant match striker, paint loss to arms, rim chip, head reattached, 7 1/4" tall.

$60+

Boy with flute
match striker, repair to basket.

$35+

Bulldog figural
match striker, 5 1/2" tall.

$175+

Bulldog figural
match striker, minor nick, hairline crack, 7" wide.

$175+

Continental Blackamoor
with straw hat atop log with baskets match striker, professional repair to feet, 7" tall.

$200+

Continental figural lion
match striker, great detail, signed "BB #2370."

$275+

Continental rabbit
and tree stump figural match striker, base repair, 8" wide.

$350+

Figural cowboy
(Rough Rider?) with rifle match striker, repair to stock of rifle, 10 1/4" tall.

$100+

Figural owl
on log match striker, 4 1/2" tall.

$150+

"HH" figural monkey
match striker, good detail, rim chips, 8" wide.

$225+

Indian figural
match striker, hairline crack, repair to feathers of Indian, 8" tall.

$50+

Man singing
with mandolin match striker, 5" tall.

$75+

Match striker
with exotic Blackamoor, English, remnant of original label, 5 1/2" tall.

$300+
Courtesy the Iridescent House

Wardle bamboo and fern
covered matchbox, repaired. (Collector tip: Wardle & Co., established 1871 at Hanley, Staffordshire, England.)

$130+

Mugs

Along with pitchers and teapots, majolica mugs are the most prone to damage. Collectors should check for handle repairs and wear to rims. And remember: Because of the lead- and tin-based glazes used in vintage majolica, these pieces should never be used for food and beverage serving or storage.

Blackberry
and floral mug.

$80+

Two mugs
various conditions.

$70+ pair

Continental Art Nouveau
lady mug, minor base nicks.

$45+

Floral and urn panel
large mug, 4 1/4" tall.

$70+

French rabbit mug
with rabbit handle, 3 1/2" tall.

$300+

Holdcroft turquoise
pond lily mug, good color, 3 1/2" tall. (Collector tip: Joseph Holdcroft majolica ware was produced at Daisy Bank in Longton, Staffordshire, England, from 1870 to 1885. Items can be found marked with "JHOLDCROFT" but many items can only be attributed by the patterns and colors that are documented to have come from the Holdcroft potteries.)

$140+

George Jones apple blossom
and basket weave mug, good color and detail, 5 1/2" tall. (Collector tip: The company started operations in the early 1860s as George Jones in Stoke, Staffordshire, England, and in 1873 became George Jones & Sons Ltd.)

$2,000+

Samuel Lear sunflower
and urn mug, nick to handle. (Collector tip: Samuel Lear, Hanley, Staffordshire, England, 1877 to 1886.)

$65+

Samuel Lear sunflower
and urn mug, hairline crack, base nick, 4" tall.

$70+

Oak leaf
and tree trunk mug.

$70+

Water lily
floral mug, good color.

$70+

Oyster Plates and Accessories

Like asparagus plates and cheese keepers, tableware related to serving oysters has become a popular collecting area in itself. This section also includes some porcelain plates.

Some majolica pieces listed here are valued in groups, and are representative of what a collector might find at large auction or private sale. Some pieces are grouped by color or style, others by use, and a few by manufacturer. The phrase "various conditions" is shorthand for a range of cracks, chips, flaking, repairs, crazing and staining. Rare or important pieces of majolica will usually have a provenance, and any repairs or restorations should be noted when they are sold.

Though assortments may offer limited information on the value of any single piece, they are an excellent place for beginning collectors to start gathering information on makers, marks, years of production and rarity.

Brown French
majolica oyster plate, 9 1/2" diameter.

$40+

Pair of black French
oyster plates with colored wells, each 9 3/4" diameter.

$110+ pair

Cobalt and lavender
crescent-shape oyster plate, outstanding color, factory glaze imperfection to one well, 10" wide.

$400+

Dark green oyster plate
with shells between wells and turquoise center, strong color, 10 1/2" diameter.

$250+

Six dark green
marble-like finish oyster plates, French, each 9 1/2" diameter.

$80+ all

CFH French porcelain
floral oyster plate, 9" wide. (Collector tip: May also be found marked "CFH/GDM for Charles Field Haviland–Gérard Dufraissiex & Morel.)

$250+

Fish oyster plate
with large fish cracker well, 10" wide.

$800+

French black
oyster platter with assorted colored wells, 13" diameter.

$60+

French dark brown
stoneware four-well oyster plate, 8" diameter.

10+

French Faience-type
oyster plate with floral center, 10 1/2" wide.

$110+

Three French
green and white basket-weave oyster plates, one with nick, each 9 1/2" diameter.

$90+ all

French green and white
basket-weave oyster tray with 12 wells, nick, 13" diameter.

$60+

French oyster plate
"St. Jean de Bretagne Décor Main." (Collector tip: The St. Jean de Bretagne pottery works are located near Quimper, France.)

$80+

Three French oyster plates
with cobalt accents, starfish in center, good detail, each 10" diameter.

$475+ all

Five French oyster plates
each 9 3/4" diameter.

$475+ all

French porcelain oyster platter
with fish and other sea creatures, 12" diameter.

$90+

French six-well
handled oyster server, cobalt ground, 13" long.

$125+

French white porcelain
oyster plate with gold trim, 9" diameter.

$40+

Gien French green
oyster plate, 9 3/4" diameter. (Collector tip: Established in the early 19th century, the Gien pottery works is located on the banks of France's Loire River near Orléans.)

$10+

Haviland Limoges
floral oyster plate, 9" diameter.

$150+

Pair of Theodore Haviland
porcelain floral oyster plates, each 9 1/2" diameter.

$250+ pair

Guillot French
oyster plate, 10 1/2" wide. (Collector tip: Guillot may be best known for its production of bird-motif plates.)

$100+

George Jones
small turquoise six-well oyster plate with raised center shell, minor crazing, 8" diameter. (Collector tip: The company started operations in the early 1860s as George Jones in Stoke, Staffordshire, England, and in 1873 became George Jones & Sons Ltd.)

$1,600+

Samuel Lear sunflower
oyster plate with lavender rim, minor rim glaze wear, 9 3/4" diameter. (Collector tip: Samuel Lear, Hanley, Staffordshire, England, 1877 to 1886.)

$1,300+

Lenox porcelain
oyster bowl with gold trim, 7 1/2" diameter.

$30+

Longchamp

small basket-weave and shell three-well oyster plate, 8" diameter. (Collector tip: Robert Charbonnier founded the Longchamp tile works in 1847 to make red clay tiles, but the factory soon started to produce majolica. Longchamp is known for its "barbotine" pieces [a paste of clay used in decorating coarse pottery in relief] made with vivid colors, especially oyster plates.)

$325+

Longchamp

oyster plate, 8 3/4" diameter.

$300

Three Longchamp

green oyster plates, each 9 3/4" diameter.

$250+ all

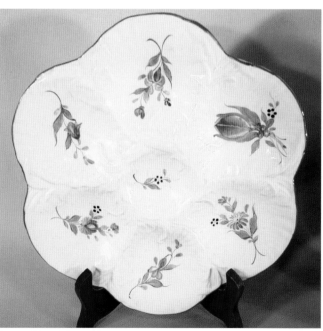

Luneville white oyster plate

with floral motif and red border, 9 1/4" diameter. (Collector tip: The Lunéville pottery was founded in 1720 by Jacques Chambrette in the city that bears its name, in the Alsace-Lorraine region of northeastern France. The firm became famous for its blue monochromatic and floral patterns. Around 1750, ceramist Paul-Louis Cyfflé introduced a pattern with animals and historical figures. Lunéville products range from hand-painted faience and Majolica to pieces influenced by the Art Deco movement.)

$25+

Lunéville
yellow and tan oyster plate, 9 1/2" diameter.

$40+

Minton fish
and seaweed oyster plate, shape no. 2366, factory rim chip under glaze, 11" diameter.

$2,000-$3,000

Minton pink
six-well oyster plate, strong color, professional rim repair, shape no. 1323, date code for 1874, 9" diameter. (Thomas Minton founded his factory in the mid-1790s in Stoke-on-Trent, Staffordshire, England. His son, Herbert Minton, introduced majolica pottery—with glazes created by Léon Arnoux—at England's Great Exhibition of 1851.)

$800+

Minton porcelain
floral oyster plate with cracker well and gold accent, 10" diameter.

$175+

Minton porcelain
floral oyster plate with cracker well and gold accent, 10" diameter.

$175+

Minton turquoise
six-well oyster plate with green center, shape no. 1323, minor rim nick to back, 9" diameter.

$375+

Minton turquoise
six-well oyster plate with green center, shape no. 1323, 9" diameter.

$425+

Minton turquoise
six-well oyster plate with green center, shape no. 1323, 9" diameter.

$425+

Minton turquoise
Six-well oyster plate with green center, shape no. 1323, 9" diameter.

$425+

Octagonal porcelain
oyster plate with brown ground, 8" wide.

$110+

Octagonal porcelain
oyster plate with blue ground, 8" wide.

$125+

Orchies gray and white
oyster plate, 9 1/2" diameter. (Collector tip: Orchies is a majolica manufacturer in northern France near Lille. It is also known under the mark "Moulin des Loups.")

$60+

Oyster plate
with alternating pink and turquoise wells and mottled center, 9 1/4" diameter.
$200+

Oyster plate
with seaweed and cobalt center, good color, 10" diameter.
$275+

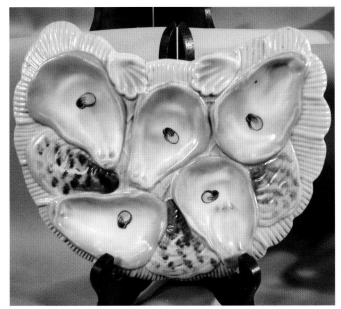

Porcelain crescent-shaped
oyster plate, factory firing hairline, 8 1/2" wide.
$250+

Pornic oyster plate
with gray ground and red/black wells, 9 3/4" diameter. (Collector tip: Faïence-rie de Pornic is located near Quimper, France.)
$10+

Pornic oyster platter
with gray ground and red and black wells, 13" diameter.

$25+

HB Quimper
large floral oyster platter, 14 1/2" diameter. (Collector tip: Named for the earliest known firm producing hand-painted pottery in Brittany, France, founded in 1685 by Jean Baptiste Bousquet.)

$125+

Henriot Quimper floral
oyster plate, 8 3/4" diameter. (Collector tip: Jules Henriot established his business in Brittany, France, in 1884 when he acquired the Dumaine works.)

$70+

Henriot Quimper floral
oyster plate, 8 3/4" diameter.

$90+

Four Henriot Quimper
individual shell oyster shells, various patterns.

$275+ all

Six shell-shaped Quimper
oyster plates, each 9" wide.

$225+ all

Pair of Quinson
French white oyster plates with green wells and yellow center, each 9 3/4"
diameter. (Collector tip: Quinson is located in Provence, France.)

$50+ pair

Reproduction Minton
fish oyster plate, 10 3/4" diameter.

$30+

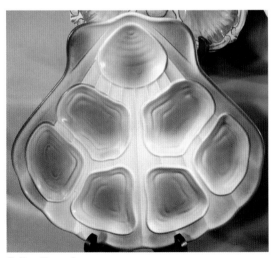

Salins French
shell-shaped oyster plate, 9 1/2" wide.

$110+

Sarreguemines dark green
oyster plate, 10" diameter. (Collector tip: Named for the city in
the Alsace-Lorraine region of northeastern France.)

$25+

Sarreguemines dark green
large oyster platter, 15" diameter.

$70+

Sarreguemines oval starfish
oyster platter and three matching oyster plates.

$400+ all

Sarreguemines oyster plate
with pink and lavender wells, green accents, 9 1/2" diameter.

$90+

Sarreguemines oyster plate
9 1/2" diameter.

$60+

Terre De Fer French
oyster plate with blue painted bird and branches, 9 3/4" diameter. (Collector tip: Terre De Fer, "Iron Ground," often associated with the Longchamp works.)

$70+

Vallauris brown and yellow
mottled oyster plate, 9" diameter. (Collector tip: Vallauris is a pottery region in southeastern France, near Cannes. Companies in production there include Massier and Foucard-Jourdan.)

$10+

Pair of Vallauris
dark green oyster plates with marble-like finish, each 9" diameter.

$90+ pair

Vallauris large green
oyster platter with marble-like finish, 14 1/2" diameter.

$60+

Vallauris large oval
brown mottled oyster platter, 11 1/2" by 18".

$70+

Victoria Pottery Co.
yellow and brown oyster plate, 10" diameter. (Collector tip: Victoria Pottery Co., Hanley, Staffordshire, England, 1895 to 1927.)

$450+

Victoria Pottery Co.
yellow oyster plate with mottled center, 10" diameter.

$400+

Wedgwood Ocean
shells and seaweed oyster plate with alternating lavender and white wells, strong color and detail, 9" diameter. (Collector tip: Founded by Josiah Wedgwood in 1759 at Burslem, Staffordshire, England.)

$800+

Wedgwood Ocean
shells and seaweed oyster plate with alternating lavender and white wells, strong color and detail, 9" diameter.

$750+

Wedgwood Ocean
shells and seaweed oyster plate with alternating lavender and white wells, strong color and detail, 9" diameter.

$1,300+

Wedgwood Ocean
shells and seaweed oyster plate with alternating lavender and white wells, strong color and detail, 9" diameter.

$800+

Wedgwood St. Louis
pattern oyster plate with cobalt and turquoise wells, strong color and detail, 9" diameter. (Collector tip: Founded by Josiah Wedgwood in 1759 at Burslem, Staffordshire, England.)

$1,300+

Pitchers

Some majolica pieces listed here are valued in groups, and are representative of what a collector might find at large auction or private sale. Some pieces are grouped by color or style, others by use, and a few by manufacturer. The phrase "various conditions" is shorthand for a range of cracks, chips, flaking, repairs, crazing and staining. Rare or important pieces of majolica will usually have a provenance, and any repairs or restorations should be noted when they are sold.

Though assortments may offer limited information on the value of any single piece, they are an excellent place for beginning collectors to start gathering information on makers, marks, years of production and rarity.

Also see jugs and ewers.

Six Baltimore Pottery Co.
pitchers, various sizes and conditions.

$140+ all

Bamboo and fern pitcher
hairline crack, rim wear, 8 1/4" tall.

$140+

Barrel-shaped floral
pewter-topped syrup pitcher, hairline crack, 4 1/2" tall.

$110+

Bevington cobalt
swan topped figural pitcher, great color, 7 1/2" tall.

$700+

Bird and leaf pitcher
with leaf spout, detailed, spout ground, 8" tall.

$350+

Bird on picket fence
pewter-topped syrup pitcher, hairline crack, 6 1/2" tall.

$110+

Bird's nest
and begonia leaf pitcher, rim repair, hairline crack, 9 1/2" tall.

$170+

Bird's nest pitcher
staining, 10" tall.

$150+

Blackberry
pewter-topped pitcher with yellow base and rim, 6" tall.

$125+

Blackberry pitcher
7 1/2" tall.

$140+

Blackberry on bark
pitcher, 7 1/2" tall.

$200+

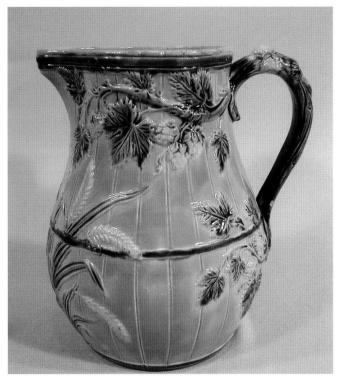

Brownfield pink
hops and wheat pitcher with lavender ground, minor glaze nick and hairline, Bacall Collection, 6 1/2" tall. (Collector tip: W. Brownfield & Son, Burslem and Cobridge, Staffordshire, England, 1850 to 1891.)

$2,300+

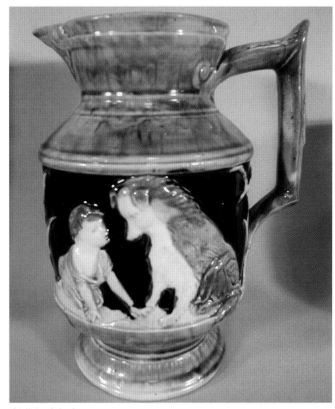

Child with dog
("Can't You Talk?") pitcher, nick to handle, 6" tall.

$150+

Cobalt child with dog
("Can't You Talk?") pitcher with pewter top, chip to handle, hairline crack to base, good color, 6 1/2" tall.

$250+

Cobalt child with dog
pitcher ("Can't You Talk?"), chip to handle, rim wear, Bacall Collection, 7" tall.

$350+

Cobalt fan
and dragonfly pitcher, nick to handle, 6 1/4" tall.

$130+

Cobalt game pitcher
French, base nick, 10 1/2" tall.

$250+

Cobalt stork
in cattails pitcher, good color, 8 1/2" tall.

$275+

Cobalt wild rose
and trellis pitcher, hairline crack, 9" tall.

$275+

Cobalt wild rose pitcher
with butterfly spout, good color, 9 1/2" tall.

$300+

Corn pitcher
minor rim nick, 8" tall.

$120+

Corn pitcher
minor spout wear, 8 1/2" tall.

$170+

Deer pitcher
and corn pitcher, various conditions.

$275+ pair

Etruscan bamboo

syrup pitcher, Bacall Collection. (Collector tip: Made by Griffen, Smith and Hill of Phoenixville, Pa., 1879 to about 1890.)

$525+

Etruscan cobalt

sunflower syrup pitcher with pewter top, lacking thumb lift, Bacall Collection.

$300+

Etruscan cobalt

sunflower syrup pitcher, lacking thumb lift on lid, strong color.

$300+

Etruscan cobalt

sunflower syrup pitcher, great color, 8" tall.

$475+

Etruscan cobalt

sunflower syrup pitcher.

$375+

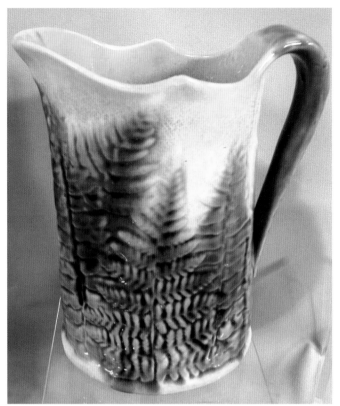

Etruscan fern pitcher
rim chips, 7" tall.

$300+

Etruscan pink
sunflower syrup pitcher, good color.

$425+

Etruscan shell
and seaweed albino pitcher, 6 1/2" tall.

$70+

Etruscan shell
and seaweed pitcher, good color, 6 1/2" tall. (Collector tip: Made by Griffen, Smith and Hill of Phoenixville, Pa., 1879 to about 1890.)

$450+

Etruscan shell
and seaweed pitcher, hairline crack, 6 3/4" tall.

$125+

Etruscan shell
and seaweed pitcher, good color, 6" tall.

$275+

Etruscan shell
and seaweed pitcher, 6" tall.

$275+

Etruscan shell
and seaweed pitcher, 4" tall.

$250+

Etruscan white
sunflower syrup pitcher.

$275+

Etruscan wild rose pitcher
with butterfly spout, minor hairline, 8" tall. (Collector tip: Made by Griffen, Smith and Hill of Phoenixville, Pa., 1879 to about 1890.)

$275+

Eureka tri-corner
owl and fan pitcher, good color, 7" tall. (Collector tip: Eureka Pottery of Trenton, N.J., circa 1883-1887.)

$160+

Two fan-and-scroll pitchers
and a fish-on-waves pitcher, various conditions.

$275+ all

Fern pattern
pewter-topped syrup pitcher, 4 1/2" tall.

$180+

Fielding fan and scroll
with insect pitcher, turquoise ground, minor surface wear to pebble ground, 6 1/2" tall. (Collector tip: Railway Pottery, established by S. Fielding & Co., Stoke, Stoke-on-Trent, Staffordshire, England, 1879.)

$110+

Fielding hummingbird
and bamboo pitcher, staining, 5 1/2" tall.

$100+

Fielding hummingbird pitcher
hairline crack, 8 1/2" tall.

$60+

Figural cockatoo pitcher
11" tall.

$325+

Set of five
figural duck pitchers.

$30+ all

Figural duck pitcher
12" tall.

$25+

Figural fish pitcher
13" tall.

$150+

Figural fish pitcher
13" tall.

$175+

Figural fish pitcher
base chip, 11 3/4" tall.

$100+

Figural fish pitcher
minor base chip, 11" tall.

$150+

Figural fish pitcher
10" tall.

$100+

Figural fish pitcher
9 3/4" tall.

$150+

Figural fish pitcher
professional spout repair, 9 1/4" tall.

$175+

Figural fish pitcher
7" tall.

$150+

Figural fish pitcher
8 1/2" tall.

$150+

Figural four-sided
fish pitcher, 7 3/4" tall.

$200+

Two figural fish pitchers
various conditions.

$140+ pair

Two figural fish pitchers
various conditions.

$130+ pair

Figural fish pitcher
11 3/4" tall.

$150+

Figural fish pitcher
10 1/4" tall.

$175+

Figural fish pitcher
10" tall.

$125+

Figural monkey pitcher
repaired, 9" tall.

$150+

Figural owl pitcher
8 1/4" tall.

$250+

Figural owl pitcher
7" tall.

$150+

Figural owl pitcher
10 1/2" tall.

$100+

Figural owl pitcher
6 1/2" tall.

$300+

Figural owl pitcher
rim wear, 6 1/2" tall, and figural parrot pitcher, base chip, 6 1/2" tall.

$150+ pair

Figural parrot pitcher
10" tall.

$225+

Figural pug dog pitcher
10 1/2" tall.

$225+

Figural seated bear pitcher
5 1/4" tall.

$50+

Figural seated bear pitcher
5 1/4" tall.

$80+

PITCHERS

Figural seated bear pitcher
7 1/2" tall.

$100+

Figural Toby pitcher
minor rim nick, 9" tall.

$110+

Flat-sided pitcher
with ship at sea, crane and fan, cobalt accents, minor hairline crack, 7 1/2" tall.

$225+

Floral ribbon
and bow pitcher, 7 1/2" tall.

$175+

Four 7" French pitchers
various conditions.

$300+ all

Four small pitchers
various conditions.

$375+ all

Four pitchers
various conditions.

$200+ all

Four pitchers
various conditions, 8" to 10" tall.

$160+ all

Five pitchers
various conditions, 7 1/2" and taller.

$250+ all

Five pitchers
various conditions.

160+ all

Four-sided floral
pewter-topped syrup pitcher, hairline crack, 4 3/4" tall.

$70+

French asparagus pitcher
minor rim wear, 8 1/4" tall.

$160+

French cat
with mandolin figural pitcher, 9 1/4" tall.

$350+

French figural
mole/rat pitcher with umbrella, professional rim repair, 8 1/2" tall.

$250+

French figural
owl pitcher, 6 3/4" tall.

$10+

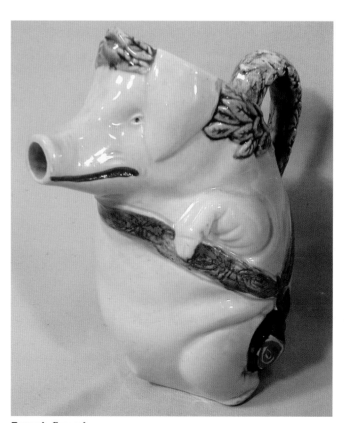

French figural
pig with ham pitcher, minor nick, 8" tall.

$225+

French rose floral pitcher
7 1/2" tall.

$125+

Frie Onnaing
"Chante Clair" figural rooster pitcher, repair to beak, 9" tall. (Collector tip: Named for the city in northern France.)

$100+

Frie Onnaing
figural "Pig Waiter" pitcher, 10 1/2" tall.

$275+

Frie Onnaing
floral pitcher, 8" tall.

$200+

Holdcroft cobalt
pond lily ice-lip pitcher, great color, 9 1/2" tall. (Collector tip: Joseph Hold-croft majolica ware was produced at Daisy Bank in Longton, Staffordshire, England, from 1870 to 1885. Items can be found marked with "JHOLD-CROFT," but many items can only be attributed by the patterns and colors that are documented to have come from the Holdcroft potteries.)

$8-$1,200

Holdcroft figural bear
with drum pitcher, professional repair to spout and rim of drum, 8 1/2" tall.

$700+

Holdcroft turquoise
pond lily pitcher, 4 3/4" tall.

$125+

George Jones bamboo pitcher
good color and detail, hairline crack, Bacall Collection, 4 3/4" tall. (Collector tip: The company started operations in the early 1860s as George Jones in Stoke, Staffordshire, England, and in 1873 became George Jones & Sons Ltd.)

$900+

George Jones pink
wheat and leaf pitcher with rope rim, professional repair to hairline crack and rim, 7 1/4" tall.

$1,400+

George Jones orchid pitcher
with leaf handle, good color, professional handle repair, 7" tall.

$1,000+

George Jones pineapple pitcher
minor glaze rim nick, good detail, Bacall Collection, 7" tall.

$450+

George Jones turquoise
apple blossom and basket pitcher, strong color and detail, Bacall Collection, 8" tall.

$1,600+

George Jones turquoise
water lily and iris pitcher, outstanding color and detail, Bacall Collection, 8 1/4" tall.

$2,500+

George Jones water lily
and iris cobalt pitcher, strong color, professional rim repair to base, 5" tall.

$1,200+

Jumbo elephant pitcher
rim wear and staining, 6 1/2" tall.

$140+

Large mottled pig pitcher
13 1/2" tall.

$15+

Minton pineapple pitcher
professional repair to spout, 9 1/4" tall. (Thomas Minton founded his factory in the mid-1790s in Stoke-on-Trent, Staffordshire, England. His son, Herbert Minton, introduced majolica pottery—with glazes created by Léon Arnoux—at England's Great Exhibition of 1851.)

$1,500

Minton pineapple pitcher
professional repair to rim and handle, 8" tall.

$500+

Morley & Co. figural
owl pitcher, base chip, 8 1/2" tall. (Morley & Co. Pottery was founded in 1879, Wellsville, Ohio, making graniteware and majolica.)

$125+

Mottled robin pitcher
with pewter top, 9 1/2" tall.

$150+

Mottled robin pitcher
9 1/2" tall.

$90+

Mottled robin
on branch pitcher, 9 1/2" tall.

$275
Courtesy of Joan Sween

Mottled shell
and anchor pitcher with fish handle, nick to handle, 4 1/2" tall.

$50+

Pewter-topped
holly and berry pitcher, 7 3/4" tall, crazing.

$50+

Picket fence
floral, ribbon and bow pitcher, good color, minor rim nick, 7" tall.

$100+

Picket fence
and floral pewter-topped syrup pitcher, 6" tall.

$110+

Picket fence
and floral pewter-topped syrup pitcher, 4" tall.

$90+

Picket fence
basket and maple leaf pewter-topped syrup pitcher, 4 3/4" tall.

$110+

Pineapple
pewter-topped syrup pitcher, 5 3/4" tall.

$150+

Pitcher
with hand holding roses, English, 7 1/2" tall, unmarked.

$450+
Courtesy the Iridescent House

Pitcher
with portrait of lady, 7 3/4" tall.

$120+

Pond lily pitcher
minor rim nick, 8 1/2" tall.

$100+

Robin on turquoise
ground pitcher, 6 3/4" tall.

$110+

St. Clement duck pitcher
13" tall. (Collector's tip: Founded by Jacques Chambrette in Saint-Clément, France, in 1758. Chambrette also established works in Luneville.)

$25+

St. Clement
duck pitcher, 13" tall.

$30+

St. Clement
rooster pitcher, 11" tall.

$30+

St. Clement
rooster pitcher, 11" tall.

$50+

Stork in marsh pitcher
with cobalt top and base, professional rim and base repair, 9" tall.

$300+

Large stork in marsh
yellow pitcher with goose-head handle, hairline crack and glaze loss, 9 3/4" tall.

$120+

Turquoise robin pitcher
rim chip, 7 1/2" tall.

$110+

Turquoise robin
on branch pitcher, 9" tall.

$400
Courtesy of Joan Sween

Turquoise tree bark
and blackberry pitcher, 4 1/2" tall.

$175+

Wardle bamboo
and fern pitcher, rim wear and nick to handle, 9" tall. (Collector tip: Wardle & Co., established 1871 at Hanley, Staffordshire, England.)

$150+

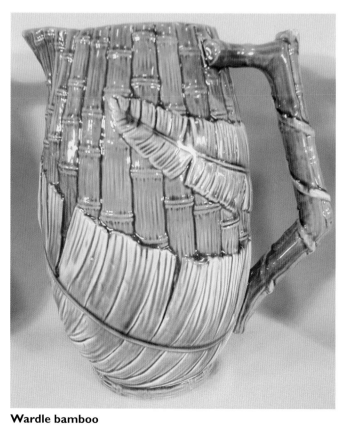

Wardle bamboo
and fern pitcher, nick to handle and rim, good color, 8 3/4" tall.

$200+

Wardle bamboo
and fern pitcher, rim and surface wear, 9" tall.

$100+

Wardle pitcher
in gathered silk and grape leaves, 7 3/8" tall.

$275
Courtesy of Joan Sween

Wedgwood Argenta
sunflower and urn pitcher, hairline crack to handle, 8" tall. (Collector tip:
Founded by Josiah Wedgwood in 1759 at Burslem, Staffordshire, England.)

$275+

Wedgwood cobalt ivy
and berry pitcher, professional rim repair, 8" tall.

$150+

Wild rose
on mottled ground pitcher, 8" tall.

$180+

Wild rose
on yellow pebble ground pitcher, small rim chip, 7 1/4" tall.

$110+

Five pitchers
various conditions, 7 1/2" and taller.

$175+ all

Six pitchers
various conditions.

$325+ all

Seven assorted pitchers
various conditions.

$300+ all

Eight assorted pitchers
various conditions.

$450+ all

Eight small pitchers
various conditions.

$450+ all

Eight pitchers
various conditions, 5 3/4".

$400+ all

Nine pitchers
various conditions, 6" and taller.

$475+ all

Nine small pitchers
various conditions.

$250+ all

Ten small assorted pitchers
various conditions.

$500+ all

Ten assorted pitchers
various conditions.

$375+ all

Place Card Holders

If the idea of a special stand for displaying place cards seems old fashioned, well, it is, but that was the mindset of the Victorian age: everything at the table had a unique use, which when taken together, created the perfect and complete dining experience.

Three Delphin Massier
floral place card holders, minor nicks to tips of flowers, each about 3 1/2" tall. (Collector tip: The Massier family began producing ceramics in Vallauris, France, in the mid-18th century.)

$1,300+ all

Three Delphin Massier
floral place card holders, minor nicks to tips of flowers, each about 3 1/2" tall.
$1,400+ all

Planters

Some majolica pieces listed here are valued in groups, and are representative of what a collector might find at large auction or private sale. Some pieces are grouped by color or style, others by use, and a few by manufacturer. The phrase "various conditions" is shorthand for a range of cracks, chips, flaking, repairs, crazing and staining. Rare or important pieces of majolica will usually have a provenance, and any repairs or restorations should be noted when they are sold.

Though assortments may offer limited information on the value of any single piece, they are an excellent place for beginning collectors to start gathering information on makers, marks, years of production and rarity.

Also see jardinières and cachepots.

Basket-weave
and floral window box planter, 10" wide.

$90+

Continental Blackamoor
figural planter of man with tambourine in front of bamboo pipes, professional repair to arm, 8 1/2" tall.

$150+

Seven Continental
figural planters, various conditions.

$120+ all

Hugo Lonitz

small dolphin footed planter with mythological faces on ends, cobalt accents, 6" wide, 5" tall. (Collector tip: Hugo Lonitz operated in Haldensleben, Germany, from 1868-1886, and later Hugo Lonitz & Co., 1886-1904, producing household and decorative porcelain and earthenware, and metal wares. Look for a mark of two entwined fish.)

$170+

Delphin Massier pair

of small figural swan planters, each 6" long, 3 1/4" tall. (Collector tip: The Massier family began producing ceramics in Vallauris, France, in the mid-18th century.)

$350+ pair

Large Delphin Massier

pink flamingo figural planter, great detail, 14 1/2" long, 10 1/2" tall.

$1,000+

Jerome Massier

figural bird planter, rim repair, 11" wide, 7" tall. (Collector tip: The Massier family began producing ceramics in Vallauris, France, in the mid-18th century.)

$50+

French Palissy Ware planter

with fish, leaves and ferns, minor rim repair, good detail, 7" wide, 5 1/2" tall. (Collector tip: In the style of Bernard Palissy, c. 1510-1590, the great French Renaissance potter.)

$400+

Sarreguemines pair

of cobalt mythological-head hanging planters with leaves and foliage in high relief, great color, shape no. 557, 11" diameter, 6" tall. (Collector tip: Named for the city in the Alsace-Lorraine region of northeastern France.)

$850+ pair

Plates

Some majolica pieces listed here are valued in groups, and are representative of what a collector might find at large auction or private sale. Some pieces are grouped by color or style, others by use, and a few by manufacturer. The phrase "various conditions" is shorthand for a range of cracks, chips, flaking, repairs, crazing and staining. Rare or important pieces of majolica will usually have a provenance, and any repairs or restorations should be noted when they are sold.

Though assortments may offer limited information on the value of any single piece, they are an excellent place for beginning collectors to start gathering information on makers, marks, years of production and rarity.

Also see dishes (assorted), platters, trays and sauce dishes.

Five assorted plates
various conditions.

$300+ all

Six assorted plates
various patterns and conditions.

$125+ all

Seven assorted plates
various conditions.

$250+ all

Eight plates
various conditions.

$275+ all

Eight dark green plates
including Wedgwood, various conditions.

$250+ all

Nine plates
various conditions.

$140+ all

Eleven majolica plates
various conditions.

$375+ all

Twelve majolica plates
various conditions.

$300+ all

Fourteen plates
various conditions, sizes starting at 8" diameter.

$500+ all

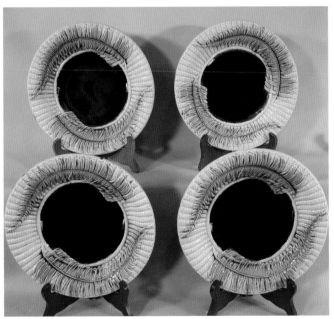

Apple and pear plate
8" diameter.

$140+

Pair of bamboo
and basket-weave plates, and begonia plate, various conditions.

$200+ all

Four bamboo
and fern plates with cobalt centers, 8 3/4", good color.

$550+ all

Begonia on basket plate
with cobalt rope edge, good color, 8" diameter.

$250+

Begonia leaf
on basket plate, minor nick, 8" diameter.

$150+

Bird plate
8" diameter.

$90+

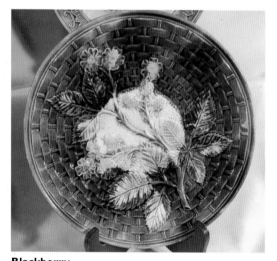

Blackberry
and basket-weave plate, minor surface wear, 9 1/4" diameter.

$50+

Blackberry
and basket-weave plate, 9 1/2" diameter.

$70+

Brown grape leaf plate
signed "Bailey Alloa," 9" diameter. (Collector's tip: The W. &
J.A. Bailey Alloa Pottery was founded in Alloa, the principal
town in Clackmannanshire, located near Edinburgh, Scotland.)

$60+

Brownfield strawberry
and leaf plate, 8 3/4" diameter. (Collector tip: W. Brownfield &
Son, Burslem and Cobridge, Staffordshire, England, 1850 to 1891.)

$275+

Butterfly and fan
on basket plate, good detail, good color, 8 1/2" diameter.

$200+

Butterfly and fan
on basket plate, good detail, rim chip to back, 8 1/2" diameter.

$70+

Choisy-le-Roi
hen and chicks plate, 8 3/4" diameter. (Collector tip: The Choisy-le-Roi faience factory of Choisy-le-Roi, France, produced majolica from 1860 until 1910.)

$100+

Choisy-le-Roi
mallard duck plate, 8 3/4" diameter.

$60+

Choisy-le-Roi
pheasant plate, 8 3/4" diameter.

$110+

Choisy-le-Roi
rabbit plate, 8 3/4" diameter.

$200+

Choisy-le-Roi
swan and cattails plate, 8 3/4" diameter.

$70+

Cobalt basket-weave
and fruit plate, 9 1/2" diameter.

$175+

Cobalt strawberry plate
strong color, 8 1/2" diameter.

$200+

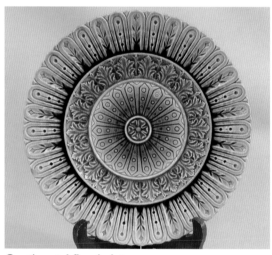

Continental floral plate
rim wear, 8 1/2" diameter.

$40+

Nine Continental plates
various patterns and conditions.

$150+ all

Deer and dog plate
8" diameter.

$110+

Deer and dog plate
9 1/4" diameter.

$100+

Deer and dog plate
9 1/4" diameter.

$100+

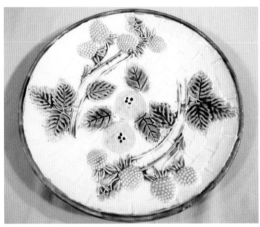

Etruscan basket-weave
strawberry and apple plate with cobalt rim, 9 1/4" diameter. (Collector tip: Made by Griffen, Smith and Hill of Phoenixville, Pa., 1879 to about 1890.)

$75+

Three Etruscan
cauliflower plates, two 9" diameter, one 8" diameter, various conditions.

$325+ all

Etruscan cauliflower plate
good color, rim chip on back, 9" diameter.

$125+

Etruscan cauliflower plate
9" diameter.

$150+

Etruscan cauliflower plate
strong color, 8" diameter.

$175+

Etruscan cobalt
basket-weave, apple and strawberry plate, 9 1/4" diameter,
good color, glaze loss.

$110+

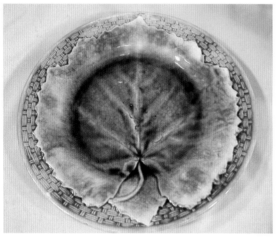

Etruscan maple leaf
on brown basket plate, 8 1/2" diameter. (Collector tip: Made by
Griffen, Smith and Hill of Phoenixville, Pa., 1879 to about 1890.)

$125+

Etruscan maple leaf
on basket plate, 9" diameter.

$125+

Etruscan maple leaf
on basket plate, 9" diameter.

$225+

Etruscan maple leaf
on basket plate, 9" diameter.

$175+

Etruscan maple leaf
on basket plate, 9" diameter.

$225+

Etruscan maple leaf
on basket plate, 9" diameter.

$225+

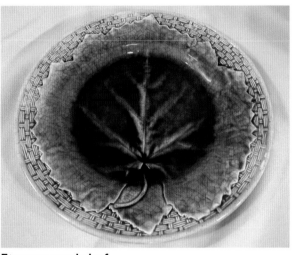

Etruscan maple leaf
on basket plate, 9" diameter.

$175+

Etruscan maple leaf
on basket plate, minor hairline crack, 8" diameter. (Collector tip: Made by Griffen, Smith and Hill of Phoenixville, Pa., 1879 to about 1890.)

$200+

Etruscan maple leaf
on pink basket plate, good color, 8" diameter.

$225+

Etruscan maple leaf
on pink basket plate, good color, 8" diameter.

$225+

Etruscan maple leaf
on pink basket plate, 8" diameter.

$225+

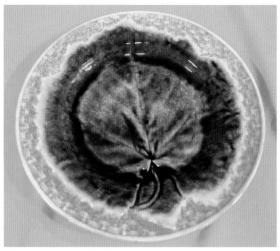

Etruscan maple leaf
on pink basket plate, strong color, 9" diameter.

$225+

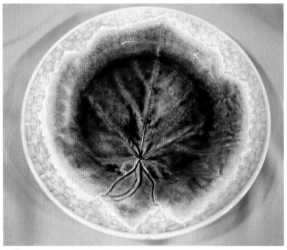

Etruscan maple leaf
on pink basket plate, 9" diameter.

$175+

Etruscan maple leaves
on pink ground plate, 9" diameter.

$125+

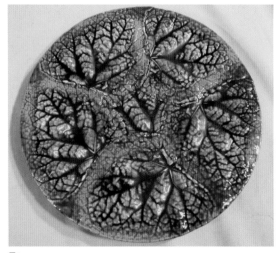

Etruscan
overlapping begonia leaf plate, 9" diameter.

$100+

Etruscan shell
and seaweed plate, hairline crack, good color, 9 1/4" diameter. (Collector tip: Made by Griffen, Smith and Hill of Phoenixville, Pa., 1879 to about 1890.)

$100+

Etruscan shell
and seaweed plate, rim chip, 9 1/4" diameter.

$150+

Pair of Etruscan
shell and seaweed 9 1/4" plates, one with hairline.

$300+ pair

Pair of Etruscan
shell and seaweed 8" plates.

$250+ pair

Pair of Etruscan
shell and seaweed 8" plates, rim nicks, hairline cracks.

$175+ pair

Etruscan shell
and seaweed plate, outstanding color, 7" diameter.

$125+

Etruscan shell
and seaweed plate, 7" diameter.

$175+

Etruscan shell
and seaweed plate, 7" diameter.

$100+

Etruscan shell
and seaweed plate, 7" diameter.

$125+

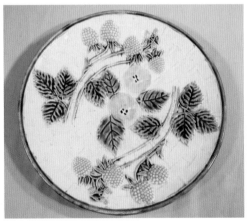

Etruscan strawberry
and apple basket-weave plate with cobalt rim, 9 1/4"
diameter. (Collector tip: Made by Griffen, Smith and Hill
of Phoenixville, Pa., 1879 to about 1890.)

$75+

Fern and floral plate
good color, 8 1/2" diameter.

$70+

Fielding bird
and fan cobalt plate, strong color, 7 1/2" diameter. (Collector tip: Railway Pottery, established by S. Fielding & Co.,
Stoke, Stoke-on-Trent, Staffordshire, England, 1879.)

$150+

Fielding bird
and fan plate, 8" diameter.

$100+

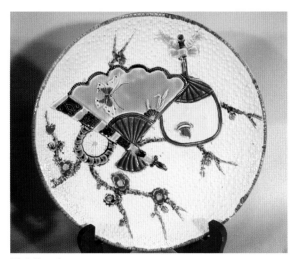

Fielding fan
and butterfly plate, 8 3/4" diameter.

$70+

Fielding morning glory
wheat, ribbon and bow plate, minor rim nick, 8" diameter.

$60+

Figural fish plate
9" wide.

$150+

Floral
leaves and fern plate 8 3/4" diameter.

$70+

Floral
leaves and fern plate, 8 3/4" diameter.

$80+

Floral and leaf plate
with wicker border and cobalt ground, good color, 8 1/2" diameter.

$250+

Fourteen French

bird and floral 8 1/4" plates and matching 8 1/2" plate in wire frame, four with hairlines.

$600+ all

French boy

on bicycle plate, 7 3/4" diameter.

$70+

French boy

on bicycle plate, 7 3/4" diameter.

$60+

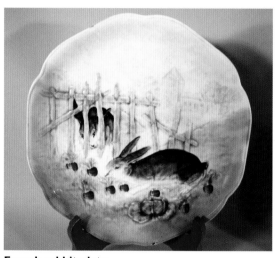

French rabbit plate

with two rabbits in garden with fence, 8 1/2" diameter.

$175+

French rooster plate
8 1/2" diameter.

$120+

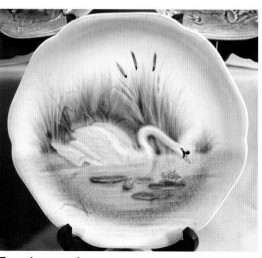

French swan plate
8 1/2" diameter.

$90+

Geranium and floral plate
with lavender flowers, strong color, 9 1/4" diameter.

$300+

Pair of German
rose plates, each 10" diameter.

$150+ pair

Seven German
turquoise bird and grape 7 1/2" plates.

$100+ all

Holdcroft cobalt leaf plate
strong color, 8 1/4" diameter. (Collector tip: Joseph Holdcroft majolica ware was produced at Daisy Bank in Longton, Staffordshire, England, from 1870 to 1885. Items can be found marked with "JHOLDCROFT," but many items can only be attributed by the patterns and colors that are documented to have come from the Holdcroft potteries.)

$385+

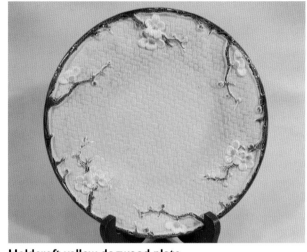

Holdcroft yellow dogwood plate
scarce to find in yellow, Bacall Collection, 8 1/2" diameter.

$700+

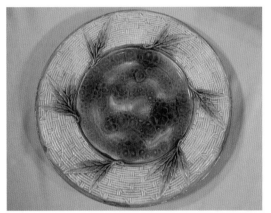

George Jones basket-weave
and bamboo plate with mottled center, strong color, rim chip, 9 1/4" diameter. (Collector tip: The company started operations in the early 1860s as George Jones in Stoke, Staffordshire, England, and in 1873 became George Jones & Sons Ltd.)

$125+

George Jones chestnut leaf
on napkin plate, minor rim wear, 9" diameter.

$225+

George Jones chestnut leaf
on napkin plate, 9" diameter.

$225+

George Jones chestnut leaf
on napkin plate, 9" diameter.

$250+

George Jones chestnut leaf
on napkin plate, 9" diameter.

$325+

George Jones chestnut leaf
and napkin plate, surface wear, 9" diameter.

$225+

George Jones leaf and ferns plate
with turquoise ground, surface wear, 8 1/2" diameter.

$200+

George Jones picket fence plate
with mottled center, 8" diameter. (Collector tip: The company started operations in the early 1860s as George Jones in Stoke, Staffordshire, England, and in 1873 became George Jones & Sons Ltd.)

$200+

George Jones pineapple plate
good color, rim chip to back, 9" diameter.

$375+

Three George Jones
pineapple plates, rim chip, surface wear, 9" diameter.

$350+ all

Samuel Lear floral and fan plate
8" diameter. (Collector tip: Samuel Lear, Hanley, Staffordshire, England, 1877 to 1886.)

$140+

Leaves and fern plate
good color, 8 1/2" diameter.

$300+

Leaves and fern plate
with turquoise ground, good color, 8 1/4" diameter.

$250+

Leaves and fern plate
with turquoise ground, minor rim glaze nicks, 8 1/2" diameter.

$175+

Maple leaf
on basket plate, good color, 9" diameter.

$100+

Morley & Co. cobalt
napkin plate, 9" diameter. (Morley & Co. Pottery was founded in 1879, Wellsville, Ohio, making graniteware and majolica.)

$90+

Minton individual
strawberry plate, great color, 8 1/2" long. (Thomas Minton founded his factory in the mid-1790s in Stoke-on-Trent, Staffordshire, England. His son, Herbert Minton, introduced majolica pottery—with glazes created by Léon Arnoux—at England's Great Exhibition of 1851.)
$700+

Minton individual
strawberry plate, strong color, hairline crack, 8 1/2" long.
$550+

Morning glory
on napkin plate with cobalt ground, 8" diameter.
$130+

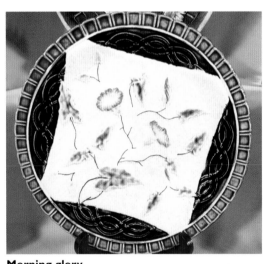

Morning glory
on napkin plate with cobalt ground, 9 1/2" diameter.
$90+

Overlapping
begonia leaf plate, 8 1/4" diameter.
$125+

Parrot on branch plate
with butterflies on border, 9" diameter.
$200+

Pineapple plate
good color, 9" diameter.

$225+

Pineapple plate
good color, 9" diameter.

$200+

Plate with image
of a dog, English, impressed "530," 6" diameter.

$200+

Courtesy the Iridescent House

Pond lily plate
8" diameter.

$150+

Plate with image
of Joan of Arc, French (?), impressed with a heart, 8 3/4" diameter.

$150+

Courtesy the Iridescent House

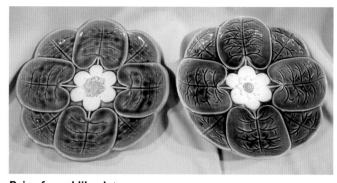

Pair of pond lily plates
one with hairline crack, each 9" diameter.

$275+ pair

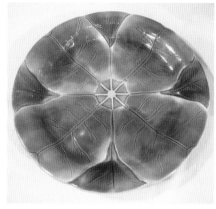

Six pond lily plates
strong color and detail, one with rim chip.

$700+ all

Pond lily plate
minor hairline crack, 9 3/4" diameter.

$125+

Twelve French Salins
lovebird and fruit 8" plates, one with hairline.

$300+ all

Ten Sarreguemines
grape plates, 7 3/4" diameter. (Collector tip: Named for the city in the Alsace-Lorraine region of northeastern France.)

$550+ all

Five stag and dog plates
various conditions.

$375+ all

Set of four Wardle
bamboo and fern plates with cobalt centers. (Collector tip: Wardle & Co., established 1871 at Hanley, Staffordshire, England.)

$250+ all

Four Wedgwood Argenta
oriental floral plates, one with hairline crack, each 8 1/4" diameter. (Collector tip: Founded by Josiah Wedgwood in 1759 at Burslem, Staffordshire, England.)

$200+ all

Wedgwood bird and fan
Argenta plate, rim nick, 8 1/4" diameter.

$50+

Wedgwood bird and fan plate
9" diameter.

$90+

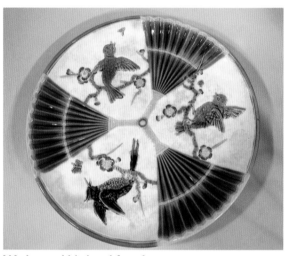

Wedgwood bird and fan plate
9" diameter.

$90+

Wedgwood cobalt
and turquoise fan and floral plate, strong color, 6 1/2" diameter.

$175+

Wedgwood cobalt lobster plate
strong color, professional rim chip repair, 8 1/2" diameter.

$4-$600

Wedgwood chrysanthemum plate
9" diameter.

$275+

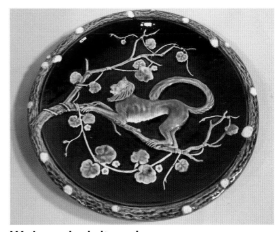

Wedgwood cobalt monkey
on branch plate, professional repair to hairline crack, 8 1/2"
diameter. (Collector tip: Founded by Josiah Wedgwood in 1759
at Burslem, Staffordshire, England.)

$850+

Wedgwood fans plate
strong color, 9" diameter.

$100+

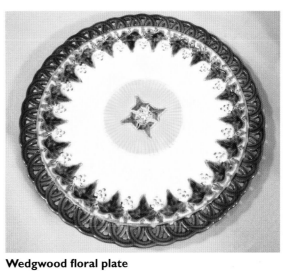

Wedgwood floral plate
with reticulated border, professional rim repair, 9" diameter.

$100+

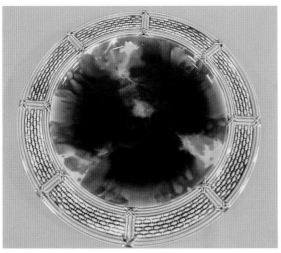

Wedgwood mottled center plate
with basket-weave edge, good color, 9" diameter.

$150+

Wedgwood grape
and leaf plate, strong color, 9" diameter.

$425+

Wedgwood Ocean plate
also impressed "IIXI," and marked with a written "2949A" under glaze, 8 1/2" diameter.

$250
Courtesy of Joan Sween

Wedgwood mottled shell plate
on three dolphin feet, 9" long. (Collector tip: Founded by Josiah Wedgwood in 1759 at Burslem, Staffordshire, England.)

$150+

Wedgwood Ocean plate
strong color and detail, 9" diameter.

$170+

Wedgwood St. Louis pattern
oriental floral plate, good color, 6 1/4" diameter.

$300+

Wedgwood triple fish
and fern plate, great color, 9" diameter.

$450+

Wedgwood turquoise
strawberry and leaf plate, 8 1/2" diameter.

$300+

Wedgwood yellow grape
and leaf plate, strong color, 9" diameter.

$350+

Wedgwood yellow grape
and leaf plate, strong color, 9" diameter. (Collector tip: Founded by Josiah Wedgwood in 1759 at Burslem, Staffordshire, England.)

$325+

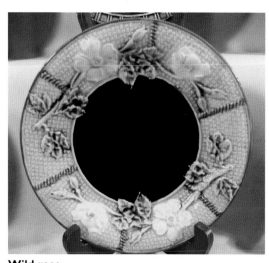

Wild rose
and rope plate with cobalt center, 7 3/4" diameter.

$65+

Wild rose
and rope plate with cobalt center, 7 3/4" diameter.

$90+

Ten plates
various conditions.

$425+ all

PLATES

Ten plates
various conditions.

$300+ all

Nine plates
various conditions.

$225+ all

Ten plates
various conditions.

$300+ all

Platters

Some majolica pieces listed here are valued in groups, and are representative of what a collector might find at large auction or private sale. Some pieces are grouped by color or style, others by use, and a few by manufacturer. The phrase "various conditions" is shorthand for a range of cracks, chips, flaking, repairs, crazing and staining. Rare or important pieces of majolica will usually have a provenance, and any repairs or restorations should be noted when they are sold.

Though assortments may offer limited information on the value of any single piece, they are an excellent place for beginning collectors to start gathering information on makers, marks, years of production and rarity.

Also see dishes (assorted), plates, trays and sauce dishes.

Bamboo platter
with cobalt center, indistinct ink stamp, and mottled-back border in brown and green, 12 3/4" wide.

$300
Courtesy of Joan Sween

Bamboo and floral platter
with cobalt center and pink ribbon and bow handles, rim chip to back, 12 3/4" wide.

$150+

Banana leaf
on bark platter, good color, 12" wide.

$190+

Banana leaf
on bark platter, minor hairline, good color.

$150+

Banana leaf
on basket platter, 14" wide.

$225+

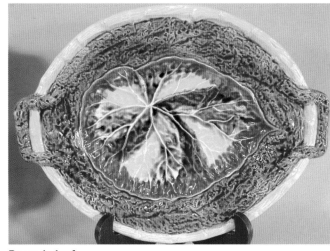

Begonia leaf
on bark platter, good color, rim chip to back, 12 1/4" wide.

$120+

Five begonia leaf platters
various conditions.

$300+ all

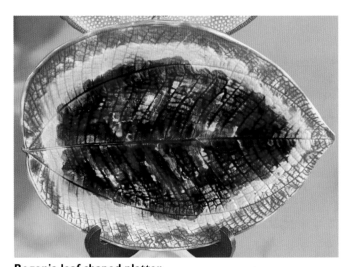

Begonia leaf-shaped platter
with pink border, good color, minor rim chip to back, 12 3/4" wide.

$250+

Bird and fan platter
16" wide.

$300+

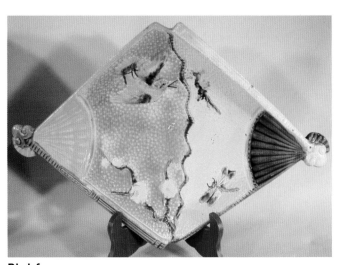

Bird, fan
and dragonfly fan platter, hairline crack, 16" wide.

$175+

Blackberry platter
with mottled center, 12" wide.

$150+

Cobalt bird
and fan platter, 11 1/2" wide.

$175+

Cobalt floral platter
strong color, 13 1/4" wide.

$250+

Cobalt wild rose platter
strong color, rim chip, hairline crack, 13" wide.

$150+

Corn platter
rim chip to back, good color, 13" wide.

$375+

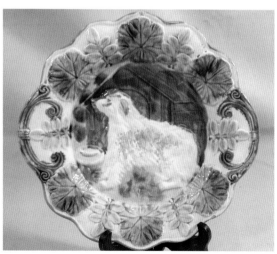

Dog and doghouse platter
rim nick, hairline, 11" diameter.

$100+

Dog and doghouse platter
11" wide.

$175+

Dog and doghouse platter
11" wide.

$250+

Dog and doghouse platter
11" wide.

$150+

Dragonfly platter
11 1/2" wide.

$110+

"Eat Thy Bread
With Thankfulness" napkin platter, professional rim repair, 15 1/4" wide.

$350+

"Eat Thy Bread
With Thankfulness" platter with fish on begonia leaf, strong detail, 12 3/4" wide.

$475+

Etruscan geranium platter
with handle, 12 1/4" wide. (Collector tip: Made by Griffen, Smith and Hill of Phoenixville, Pa., 1879 to about 1890.)

$200
Courtesy of Joan Sween

Etruscan geranium platter
minor hairline crack to handle, 12" wide.

$150+

Etruscan geranium platter
12" wide.

$175+

Etruscan shell
and seaweed platter, minor rim nicks, 13" wide.

$350+

Fielding fan and insect
with scroll platter with turquoise pebble ground, good color, minor rim chip to back, 13" wide. (Collector tip: Railway Pottery, established by S. Fielding & Co., Stoke, Stoke-on-Trent, Staffordshire, England, 1879.)

$200+

Geranium platter
with lavender flowers, outstanding color and detail, 12" wide.

$550+

George Jones overlapping
ferns and leaves platter with twig handles, strong color and detail, 14" wide. (Collector tip: The company started operations in the early 1860s as George Jones in Stoke, Staffordshire, England, and in 1873 became George Jones & Sons Ltd.)

$2,300+

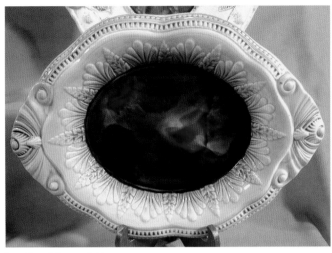

Leaf and fern platter
with mottled center and lavender border, good color, 14" wide.

$250+

Leaves and fern platter
with turquoise ground, 12 1/4" wide.

$325+

Leaves and fern platter
with yellow ground, 12 1/4" wide.

$250+

Minton floral charger
or platter, factory firing hairline, professional rim repair, 14" diameter. (Thomas Minton founded his factory in the mid-1790s in Stoke-on-Trent, Staffordshire, England. His son, Herbert Minton, introduced majolica pottery—with glazes created by Léon Arnoux—at England's Great Exhibition of 1851.)

$300

Minton Palissy-style platter
professional hairline crack repair to center, 15" wide.

$200+

Pear and leaf platter
good color, 13" wide.

$325+

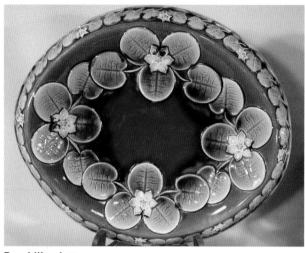

Pond lily platter
strong color, 13" wide.

$400+

Toby with mug platter
11" diameter.

$25+

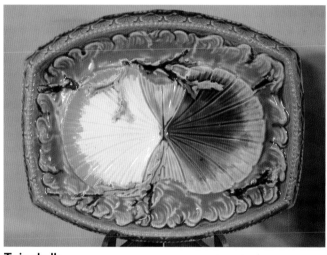

Twin shells
on waves platter with shell border, 12 3/4" wide.

$375+

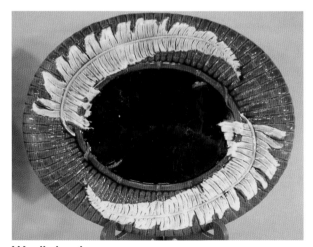

Wardle bamboo
and fern platter with cobalt center, 13" wide. (Collector tip: Wardle &
Co., established 1871 at Hanley, Staffordshire, England.)

$250+

Wardle bird
and fan with bamboo oval platter, crazing, 12 1/2" wide.

$110+

Wedgwood Argenta
corn and poppy platter, 13" wide. (Collector tip: Founded by Josiah Wedgwood in 1759 at Burslem, Staffordshire, England.)

$325+

Wedgwood Argenta
Ocean platter, hairline and base chip.

$160+

Wedgwood Argenta
sunflower and begonia leaf platter, 11" wide.

$150+

Wedgwood cobalt
cycle and wheat harvest platter, professional rim repair, 13" diameter.

$300+

Wedgwood platter
with lady and serpent in the sea, good color and detail, professional rim repair, 15" tall.

$600-$900

Wedgwood
St. Louis-pattern platter, good color, hairline crack, 12" tall.

$500-$750

Wedgwood yellow
salmon platter, extremely rare in this color, outstanding color, detail and condition, 25" long, 12 3/4" wide. (Collector tip: Founded by Josiah Wedgwood in 1759 at Burslem, Staffordshire, England.)

$12,500+

Wild rose platter
with turquoise ground, crazing, 13 1/2" wide.

$200+

Four platters
various conditions.

$200+ all

Four platters
various conditions.

$150+ all

Four platters
various conditions.

$300+ all

Four platters
various conditions.

$475+ all

Plaques

Majolica plaques range from simple plate-size examples to imposing (more than 30 in. diameter) Italian-influenced pieces similar to those produced in Faenza in the 15th century.

Jose Cunha Portugal
Palissy plaque with snake, lizard and other creatures on bed of heavy grass, 9 1/2" diameter. (Collector tip: Jose A. Cunha, Caldas da Rainha, southern Portugal, worked in the style of Bernard Palissy, the great French Renaissance potter.)

$650+

French Maurice
Palissy Ware lobster plaque, cobalt ground, great color, professional repair to back rim and to lobster's head, 15 1/2" long. (Collector tip: François Maurice, School of Paris, active 1875-85, worked in the style of Bernard Palissy, c. 1510-1590, the great French Renaissance potter.)

$2,000

George Morley fish
wall plaque, rim repair to back, 13 1/2" long. (George Morley & Co., East Liverpool, Ohio, 1884 to 1891.)

$175+

Punch Bowls

Not all punch bowls are as exuberantly whimsical as the "Punch" creation seen here, but even the simplest designs can still command strong prices. A bowl in the pond lily pattern with cobalt ground by Griffen, Smith and Hill of Phoenixville, Pa., might cost $2,000. Individual cups can sell for $150 and up.

George Jones "Punch"
punch bowl with turquoise ground, professional rim, hat and leg repair, great detail, hard to find in turquoise, 11" diameter, 8 1/4" tall. (Collector tip: The company started operations in the early 1860s as George Jones in Stoke, Staffordshire, England, and in 1873 became George Jones & Sons Ltd.)

$15,000+

Wedgwood grape
and vine punch set with large punch bowl, 10 1/2" diameter, 6 1/2" tall, and eight matching cups, strong color and detail to entire set, rare to find a complete set. (Collector tip: Founded by Josiah Wedgwood in 1759 at Burslem, Staffordshire, England.)

$1,500

Salts

Like oyster plates, tableware related to serving salt has become a popular collecting area in itself.

Some majolica pieces listed here are valued in groups, and are representative of what a collector might find at large auction or private sale. Some pieces are grouped by color or style, others by use, and a few by manufacturer. The phrase "various conditions" is shorthand for a range of cracks, chips, flaking, repairs, crazing and staining. Rare or important pieces of majolica will usually have a provenance, and any repairs or restorations should be noted when they are sold.

Though assortments may offer limited information on the value of any single piece, they are an excellent place for beginning collectors to start gathering information on makers, marks, years of production and rarity.

Pair of Etruscan lily salts
nicks and repair. (Collector tip: Made by Griffen, Smith and Hill of Phoenixville, Pa., 1879 to about 1890.)

$60+ pair

French hen
and rooster figural double salt, each 3 1/2" tall.

$175+ pair

French hen
and rooster figural double salt, each 3 1/2" tall.

$175+ pair

Thomas Sergent pair
of figural chicken double salts, rim nicks and repairs, unusual form, each 4" wide. (Collector tip: Thomas-Victor Sergent was one of the School of Paris ceramists of the late 19th century who were influenced by the works of Bernard Palissy, c. 1510-1590, the great French Renaissance potter.)

$275+ pair

Two-compartment lemon
figural salt, attributed to Massier, 4" tall.

$125+

Sardine Boxes

If the idea of a special vessel for serving sardines seems old fashioned, well, it is, but that was the mindset of the Victorian age: everything at the table had a unique use, which when taken together, created the perfect and complete dining experience.

Albino lobster
covered sardine box.

$60+

Basket-weave
sardine box with pineapple lid.

$275+

Lot Brown
sardine box with attached under plate and overlapping fish on lid, minor rim chip to box.

$200+

Cobalt sardine box
with attached under plate, fish on bed of seaweed on cover, rim chips to lid, hairline crack to base.

$250+

George Jones cobalt
pointed-leaves sardine box and tray, repair to corner of lid. (Collector tip: The company started operations in the early 1860s as George Jones in Stoke, Staffordshire, England, and in 1873 became George Jones & Sons Ltd.)

$700+

George Jones cobalt
pointed-leaves sardine box and tray, no cover, chip to tray.

$100+

George Jones pointed-leaves
sardine box with tray, good color, rim repair to lid.

$750+

Wilhelm Schiller and Sons
(W.S. & S.) picket fence mottled sardine box with fish on cover, attached under plate, good color. (Collector tip: Wilhelm Schiller and Sons, Bodenbach, Bohemia, established 1885.)

$150+

Yellow sardine box
with attached under plate.

$200+

Sauce Dishes

Some majolica pieces listed here are valued in groups, and are representative of what a collector might find at large auction or private sale. Some pieces are grouped by color or style, others by use, and a few by manufacturer. The phrase "various conditions" is shorthand for a range of cracks, chips, flaking, repairs, crazing and staining. Rare or important pieces of majolica will usually have a provenance, and any repairs or restorations should be noted when they are sold.

Though assortments may offer limited information on the value of any single piece, they are an excellent place for beginning collectors to start gathering information on makers, marks, years of production and rarity.

Five basket-weave
floral and leaf sauce dishes, each 5 1/2" diameter, wear, one with hairline, nicks.

$50+ all

Pair of dragonfly
and fan sauce dishes, one with yellow ground and one with turquoise.

$150+ pair

Etruscan cobalt
sunflower sauce dish, strong color, 5" diameter. (Collector tip: Made by Griffen, Smith and Hill of Phoenixville, Pa., 1879 to about 1890.)

$250+

Three Etruscan
shell and seaweed scalloped-edge sauce dishes, minor nicks.

$325+ all

Etruscan shell
and seaweed shell-shaped sauce dish.

$110+

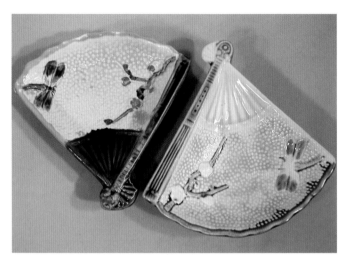

Pair of fan-shaped
dragonfly sauce dishes, each 6 1/2" long.

$150+ pair

Pair of water sauce dishes
with shell handles, each with minor rim nicks.

$100+ pair

Wedgwood ribbon
and bow sauce dish, 7" wide. (Collector tip: Founded by Josiah Wedgwood in 1759 at Burslem, Staffordshire, England.)

$150+

Servers

All of the servers in this section have raised or applied figural decorations, and a few come with small accessory pieces, so collectors should look closely for signs of repair or touchups.

Begonia leaf
double server with stork handle, professional repair to top of stork's head, 11 3/4" wide.

$100+

Figural
double begonia leaf server with stork handle, head reattached, rim repair.

$75+

Bird and holly
figural server, professional repair to bird, 8 1/4" wide.

$350+

Choisy-le-Roi
twig-handled double server, professional rim repair, 11 1/2" wide. (Collector tip: The Choisy-le-Roi faience factory of Choisy-le-Roi, France, produced majolica from 1860 until 1910.)

$100+

Holdcroft double-shell
owl server, great detail, rare with owl center handle, professional repair to shell, 16" wide, 8 1/2" tall. (Collector tip: Joseph Holdcroft majolica ware was produced at Daisy Bank in Longton, Staffordshire, England, from 1870 to 1885. Items can be found marked with "JHOLDCROFT" but many items can only be attributed by the patterns and colors that are documented to have come from the Holdcroft potteries.)

$2,500+

Holdcroft turquoise
strawberry server with twig handles, professional handle repair, 11 1/2" long.
$400+

George Jones bird
on leaf server, good color, lacking bird. (Collector tip: The company started operations in the early 1860s as George Jones in Stoke, Staffordshire, England, and in 1873 became George Jones & Sons Ltd.)
$100+

George Jones bird
on floral tray strawberry server with cream and sugar, strong color and detail, professional repair to bird's beak, 11" wide.
$1,800+

George Jones cobalt
basket-weave and leaves double server with twig handle, paint loss to rim, 13" wide.
$225+

George Jones strawberry server
with cream and sugar, strong color and detail, 14 1/2" long.
$1,500-$2,000

George Jones yellow
basket-weave strawberry server, good color, minor rim glaze flakes, 9" long.

$700+

Minton chestnut server
shape no. 594, professional repair to tip of leaf, 9 1/2" diameter. (Thomas Minton founded his factory in the mid-1790s in Stoke-on-Trent, Staffordshire, England. His son, Herbert Minton, introduced majolica pottery—with glazes created by Léon Arnoux—at England's Great Exhibition of 1851.)

$400+

Minton triple-shell
seafood condiment server with shell handle, rare form, shape no. 1557, date code for 1870, minor rim chips to shell, 5 1/2" tall, 8" wide.

$2,300+

Turquoise strawberry server
with flowers and leaves, twig handle and attached cream and sugar bowls, good color, 10" diameter.

$225+

Shelves

Majolica shelves are quite rare, especially figural examples like those by Sargent shown here, which have distinct left and right versions.

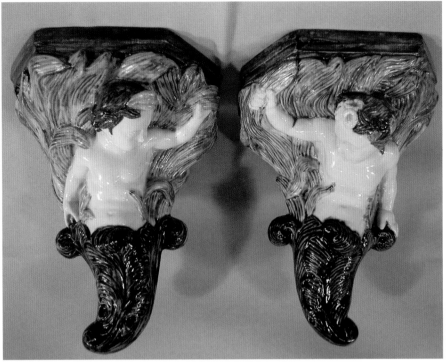

Thomas Sergent
pair of wall bracket shelves with boy and girl puttis among leaves, professional rim repair to shelves, 9 1/2" tall, 7 1/2" wide. (Collector tip: Thomas-Victor Sergent was one of the School of Paris ceramists of the late 19th century who was influenced by the works of Bernard Palissy, c. 1510-1590, the great French Renaissance potter.)

$900+ pair

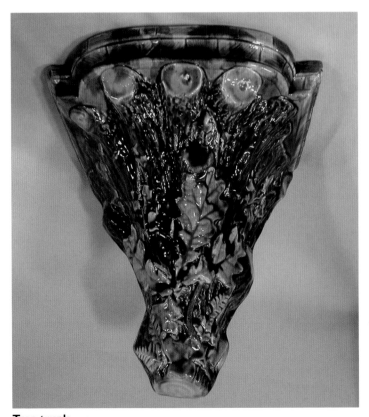

Tree trunk
and oak leaf wall bracket shelf, minor nicks, 9" tall, 8 1/2" wide.

$500+

Spooners

Victorian-era table settings often included a spooner, meant to hold spoons. The spooner is the shorter of two vase-shaped items, and the celery vase is the taller.

Bird and fan spooner
rim glaze wear, 5" tall.

$100+

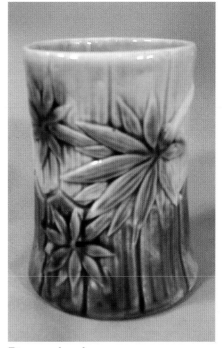

Etruscan bamboo spooner
4 1/4" tall. (Collector tip: Made by Griffen, Smith and Hill of Phoenixville, Pa., 1879 to about 1890.)

$475+

Floral
and basket-weave spooner, good color, 4 1/2" tall.

$125+

Holdcroft dogwood
turquoise spooner, rim glaze wear, 5" tall. (Collector tip: Joseph Holdcroft majolica ware was produced at Daisy Bank in Longton, Staffordshire, England, from 1870 to 1885. Items can be found marked with "JHOLDCROFT," but many items can only be attributed by the patterns and colors that are documented to have come from the Holdcroft potteries.)

$75+

Samuel Lear
water lily spooner, 5 1/4" tall. (Collector tip: Samuel Lear, Hanley, Staffordshire, England, 1877 to 1886.)

$115+

Teapots

Along with pitchers and mugs, majolica teapots are the most prone to damage. Collectors should check for handle repairs and wear to spouts. And remember: Because of the lead- and tin-based glazes used in vintage majolica, these pieces should never be used for food and beverage serving or storage.

Bird and bird's nest
figural teapot, professional minor spout repair, 9 1/2" long, 5 1/4" tall.

$300+

Birds
in flight teapot, 6" tall.

$175+

Blackberry teapot
spout chip, 6 1/2" tall.

$175+

Cobalt Chinaman teapot
good color, professional spout repair, 8 1/2" long, 6 1/4" tall.

$300+

Cobalt teapot
with butterfly handle on lid, and birds and fans in relief on side, good color, professional spout repair, 9 1/2" long, 5 1/2" tall.

$225+

Etruscan large shell
and seaweed teapot with crooked spout, good color. (Collector tip: Made by Griffen, Smith and Hill of Phoenixville, Pa., 1879 to about 1890.)

$500+

Etruscan large shell
and seaweed teapot with crooked spout, hairline crack.

$400+

Etruscan shell
and seaweed small teapot with crooked spout, nick to spout, 5 1/2" tall.

$375+

Etruscan small shell
and seaweed teapot with straight spout, minor nicks and hairline crack to inside of lid.

$350+

Fielding fan and scroll
with insect teapot, chip to lid finial. (Collector tip: Railway Pottery, established by S. Fielding & Co., Stoke, Stoke-on-Trent, Staffordshire, England, 1879.)

$200+

Fielding ribbon
bow, daisy and wheat teapot, great detail, 6" tall.

$350+

Holdcroft Chinaman

and coconut figural teapot and matching creamer, minor professional rim repair to lid and rim of teapot, 7" tall, 10 1/2" long. (Collector tip: Joseph Holdcroft majolica ware was produced at Daisy Bank in Longton, Staffordshire, England, from 1870 to 1885. Items can be found marked with "JHOLDCROFT," but many items can only be attributed by the patterns and colors that are documented to have come from the Holdcroft potteries.)

$600+ pair

Minton monkey

and coconut figural teapot, strong color and detail, minor hairline crack to spout, 8 1/2" long, 6" tall. (Thomas Minton founded his factory in the mid-1790s in Stoke-on-Trent, Staffordshire, England. His son, Herbert Minton, introduced majolica pottery—with glazes created by Léon Arnoux—at England's Great Exhibition of 1851.)

$5,750+

Minton "Spikey" fish

figural teapot, extremely rare, professional repair to spout, base rim and rim of lid, outstanding color and detail, 9 1/2" long, 7" tall.

$26,000+

Pineapple teapot

strong color, good detail, repair to rim of lid, 6 1/2" tall.

$350+

J. Roth figural

cobalt monkey-handle teapot, strong color, 10" long, 7 1/4" tall. (Roth was a London potter active in the 1880s.)

$3,300+

Royal Doulton

limited-edition Minton Chinaman teapot.

$200+

Royal Doulton
limited-edition Minton Fish teapot.

$550+

Royal Worcester
dragon-handled teapot with birds, flowers and vine in relief, strong color and detail, minor professional spout repair, rare, 7 1/2" tall.

$3,000+

Sailor on coil of rope
three-legged figural teapot, Isle of Man, professional repair to spout, legs and base, good color, 9 3/4" tall.

$400+

Shorter and Bolton
bird and fan teapot, hairline crack to spout, 8 1/2" tall.

$250+

Wardle bamboo
and fern teapot and under plate, rim chips to plate. (Collector tip: Wardle & Co., established 1871 at Hanley, Staffordshire, England.)

$275+ set

Wild rose
and rope teapot, minor rim nick to pot, 7 1/4" tall.

$150+

Yellow basket-weave
and berry teapot, spout nick.

$175+

Tea Sets

Along with pitchers and mugs, majolica tea sets are the most prone to damage. Collectors should check for handle repairs and wear to rims and spouts. And remember: Because of the lead- and tin-based glazes used in vintage majolica, these pieces should never be used for food and beverage serving or storage.

Basket-weave
and floral three-piece tea set, rim chip to creamer.

$175+ all

Bird and fan teapot
and matching sugar, nick to spout of teapot, rim chip to lid of sugar.

$100+ pair

Bird and fan
on pebble ground three-piece tea set, strong color, minor spout chip to teapot.

$275+ all

Blackberry
and basket-weave teapot and sugar with cobalt ground, base chip to pot, lid rim repair and handle repair to sugar.

$175+ pair

Child's 19-piece tea set
with teapot, creamer, sugars, plates, cups and saucers, white with floral motif, various conditions.

$160+ all

Cranes in flight
three-piece tea set, minor glaze nicks.

$150+ all

Etruscan cauliflower
three-piece tea set, glaze loss to inside of teapot lid and nick to spout. (Collector tip: Made by Griffen, Smith and Hill of Phoenixville, Pa., 1879 to about 1890.)

$350+ all

Etruscan cauliflower
three-piece tea set, minor nicks to all three pieces.

$350+ all

French 11-piece
brown mottled tea set, various conditions.

$50+ all

George Jones cobalt
drum-shape three-piece tea set with strap and buckle handles, drum stick spout on teapot, outstanding color and detail, very rare set, teapot 6" tall. (Collector tip: The company started operations in the early 1860s as George Jones in Stoke, Staffordshire, England, and in 1873 became George Jones & Sons Ltd.)

$11,000 set

Samuel Lear water lily
three-piece tea set, various conditions. (Collector tip: Samuel Lear, Hanley, Staffordshire, England, 1877 to 1886.)

$100+ all

Lovebirds and floral
three-piece tea set, minor glaze nick to spout of teapot, sugar lid lacking handle.

$75+ all

Clement Massier
seven-piece tea set with teapot, creamer, sugar, and two cups and saucers with floral and dragonfly motif. (Collector tip: The Massier family began producing ceramics in Vallauris, France, in the mid-18th century.)

$300+ all

Turquoise floral
three-piece tea set, hairline crack to creamer.

$325+ all

Victoria Pottery Co.
(VPC) floral three-piece tea set, professional spout repair to creamer. (Collector tip: The Victoria Pottery Co. of Hanley, Staffordshire, England, was active from 1895 to the late 1920s.)

$700+ all

Wardle bamboo
and fern teapot, pitcher and sugar, minor nicks to teapot, mismatched lid on sugar. (Collector tip: Wardle & Co., established 1871 at Hanley, Staffordshire, England.)

$275+ all

Tiles

The tiles seen here are sometimes called tea tiles since they were intended for use under a hot teapot. Decorative wall-mounted tiles from the 19th century are still being salvaged from homes in the U.K. and Europe. An excellent resource for these tiles is Tile Heaven, www.tile-heaven.co.uk.

Dog tile
in wire trivet frame, 6" square.

$75+

George Jones twig
and ivy footed tea tile with portrait in center, unusual form, 7" diameter. (Collector tip: The company started operations in the early 1860s as George Jones in Stoke, Staffordshire, England, and in 1873 became George Jones & Sons Ltd.)

$100+

Puppy tile
in wire trivet frame, 6" square.

$60+

Toothpick Holders

Simple majolica toothpick holders — even those by known makers like Schiller & Sons — can still be found for under $50.

Continental chicken
with barrel figural toothpick holder, good detail, 4 3/4" tall.

$100+

Moth and butterfly
toothpick holder, good color, 1 3/4" tall.

$190+

W.S. & S. cobalt
deer and trees toothpick holder, rim chip, 2" tall. (Collector tip: Wilhelm Schiller & Sons, Bodenbach, Bohemia, established 1885.)

$50+

Trays

Some majolica pieces listed here are valued in groups, and are representative of what a collector might find at large auction or private sale. Some pieces are grouped by color or style, others by use, and a few by manufacturer. The phrase "various conditions" is shorthand for a range of cracks, chips, flaking, repairs, crazing and staining. Rare or important pieces of majolica will usually have a provenance, and any repairs or restorations should be noted when they are sold.

Though assortments may offer limited information on the value of any single piece, they are an excellent place for beginning collectors to start gathering information on makers, marks, years of production and rarity.

Also see dishes (assorted), plates, platters and sauce dishes.

Pair of begonia leaf trays

$175+ pair

Three begonia leaf trays
various conditions.

$275+ all

Three begonia leaf trays

$250+ all

Three begonia leaf trays

$250+ all

Three begonia leaf trays

$375+ all

Eight begonia leaf trays
excellent examples, various conditions.

$600+ all

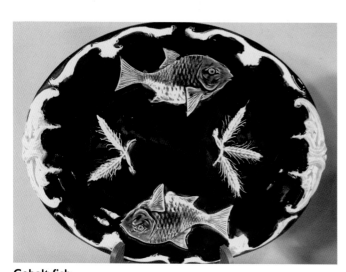

Cobalt fish
and seaweed tray, strong color and detail, 13 1/2" wide.

$450+

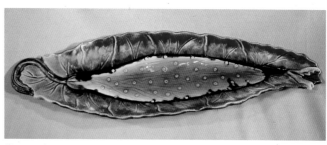

Cucumber tray
good color, 16 1/2" long.

$40+

"Eat Thy Bread
With Thankfulness" begonia bread tray, 13" wide.

$250+

"Eat Thy Bread
With Thankfulness" wheat bread tray, rim chips.

$170+

Four Etruscan
begonia leaf trays various conditions. (Collector tip: Made by Griffen, Smith and Hill of Phoenixville, Pa., 1879 to about 1890.)

$250+ all

Five large Etruscan
begonia leaf trays, various conditions.

$325+ all

Five large Etruscan
begonia leaf trays, various conditions.

$325+ all

Six small Etruscan
begonia leaf trays, various conditions.

$425+ all

Etruscan geranium tray
12" wide.

$175+

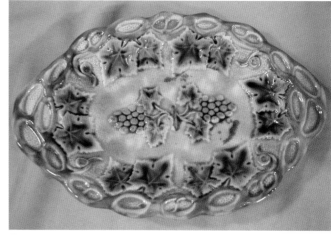

Etruscan pink grape tray
good color, minor rim nick to back, 10" wide.

$175+

Etruscan pink grape tray
rim nicks, 10" wide. (Collector tip: Made by Griffen, Smith and Hill of Phoenixville, Pa., 1879 to about 1890.)

$150+

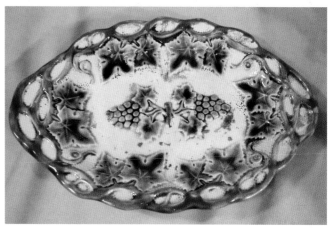

Etruscan grape tray
with white ground, 10" wide.

$150+

Etruscan oak leaf tray
12" wide.

$175+

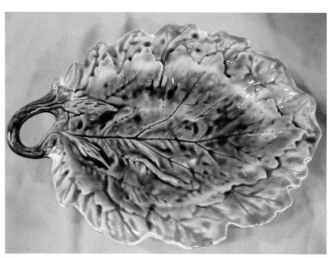

Etruscan oak leaf tray
with pink border, good color.

$200+

Etruscan oak leaf tray
with salmon pink border, 12" wide.

$200+

Etruscan oak leaf tray
with yellow border, 12" wide. (Collector tip: Made by Griffen, Smith and Hill of Phoenixville, Pa., 1879 to about 1890.)

$175+

Large fan-shaped
dragonfly and fan tray, 10 1/2" long.

$175+

Fan-shaped
dragonfly tray with cobalt ribbon handle, 10" long.

$225+

Pair of fan-shaped
floral trays with ribbon handle, rim nick to one, each 6 1/2" long.

$110+ pair

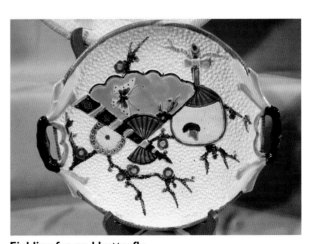

Fielding fan and butterfly
two-handled tray, good color, 10 1/2" wide. (Collector tip: Railway Pottery, established by S. Fielding & Co., Stoke, Stoke-on-Trent, Staffordshire, England, 1879.)

$180+

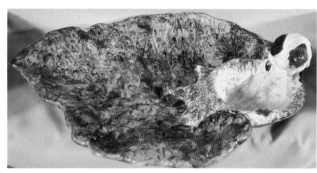

Figural tray
with bird on rim of begonia leaf, 14" long.

$15+

Fielding fan-shaped tray
with heron and feet in the shape of shells, crazing, 10 1/2" long.

$380
Courtesy of Joan Sween

French placement tray
with yellow rope trim and red tassels, 12 1/2" wide.

$60+

George Jones chestnut leaf tray
with mottled center, hairline, 12" diameter. (Collector tip: The company started operations in the early 1860s as George Jones in Stoke, Staffordshire, England, and in 1873 became George Jones & Sons Ltd.)

$400+

George Jones cobalt
basket-weave tray with yellow rope border and green floral center, minor professional rim repair, 10 1/4" diameter.

$350+

George Jones cobalt
butterfly, wheat and bamboo tray, outstanding color and detail, 13" wide.
$2,800+

George Jones thrush on leaf
and floral tray with rare pink ground, strong color and detail, bird professionally reattached, 10" wide.
$2,500+

George Jones turquoise
butterfly, wheat and bamboo two-handled tray, outstanding color and detail, Bacall Collection, 13" wide.
$4,000+

George Jones turquoise
leaf tray with twig handle, lacking bird or squirrel, twigs professionally restored into handle, strong color, 10 1/4" wide. (Collector tip: The company started operations in the early 1860s as George Jones in Stoke, Staffordshire, England, and in 1873 became George Jones & Sons Ltd.)
$350+

Three leaf trays
various conditions.
$100+ all

Four leaf trays
various conditions.
$150+ all

Five leaf trays
various conditions.

$130+ all

Six leaf trays
various conditions.

$145+ all

Samuel Lear classical urn
and sunflower tray with yellow rim, rim nick, 14" wide. (Collector tip: Samuel Lear, Hanley, Staffordshire, England, 1877 to 1886.)

$250+

Longchamp lobster tray
strong color and detail, 14 1/2" wide. (Collector tip: Robert Charbonnier founded the Longchamp tile works in 1847 to make red clay tiles, but the factory soon started to produce majolica. Longchamp is known for its "barbotine" pieces [a paste of clay used in decorating coarse pottery in relief] made with vivid colors, especially oyster plates.)

$1,100+

Minton cucumber tray
very rare and unusual form, date code for 1871, shape no. 1572, professional rim repair, 15" long.

$6-$900

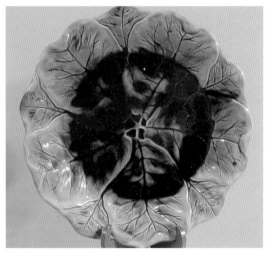

Minton dark green
pond lily round tray or under plate, 14" diameter.

$100+

Minton oak leaf tray
with birds on branch at each end with acorns, each bird's head is a lid which lifts off to create an inkwell or preserve pots, great color and detail, shape no. 1458, date code for 1870, nick to one lid, Bacall Collection, 13" long.

$2,500+

George Morley fish tray
13" long. (George Morley & Co., East Liverpool, Ohio, 1884 to 1891.)

$150+

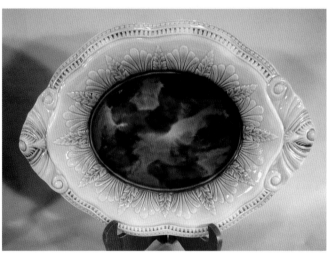

Mottled-center tray
with lavender accent, 14" wide.

$275+

Mottled leaf
and fern tray with lavender border, 14" wide.

$275+

Seven novelty leaf trays
with pipes, dice and biscuits, various conditions.

$65+ all

HB Quimper tear-drop shape tray
with floral motif, 8" long. (Collector tip: Named for the earliest known firm producing hand-painted pottery in Brittany, France, founded in 1685 by Jean Baptiste Bousquet.)

$50+

HB Quimper tear-drop shape
floral tray with serving knife, tray 7 1/2" long.

$60+ pair

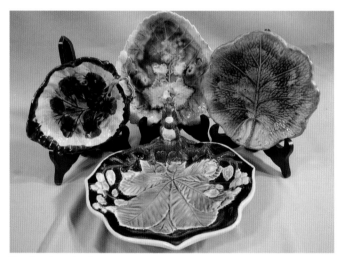

Squirrel on leaf tray
and three leaf trays, various conditions.

$100+ all

Squirrel with nut
on leaf tray, rim repair, hairline crack.

$135+

Wedgwood cobalt
bird and pond lily serving tray, strong color and detail, 9 3/4" wide. (Collector tip: Founded by Josiah Wedgwood in 1759 at Burslem, Staffordshire, England.)

$900+

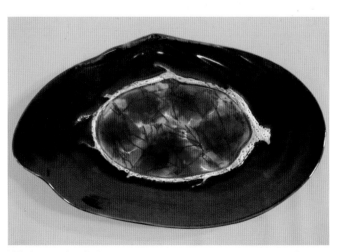

Wedgwood cobalt
shell shaped tray with mottled center, 12" long.

$100+

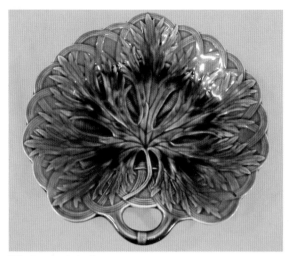

Wedgwood dark green
leaf and wicker handled tray, 9 1/2" long.

$130+

Wedgwood heart-shaped
vegetable tray, unusual form, 7" long.

$90+

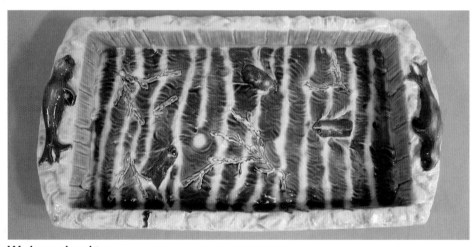

Wedgwood seal tray
with seal handles and seals swimming in base with seaweed, great detail, professional rim repair, 16 3/4" wide.

$400+

Wedgwood turquoise
basket-weave grape tray with twig handles, 9 1/2" diameter. (Collector tip: Founded by Josiah Wedgwood in 1759 at Burslem, Staffordshire, England.)

$400+

"Where Reason Rules
The Appetite Obeys" wheat bread tray, 12 1/2" wide.

$350+

Tureens

It's worth noting that while vintage majolica tureens like those seen here can sell for more than $1,000 in excellent condition, the contemporary pieces being produced in limited editions today are selling for even more.

Brownfield tureen
with bull, horse and calf head handles, with under plate, hairline crack to base, rim chip to tray and lid handle, 9" wide. (Collector tip: William Brownfield wares, made at Burslem, Stoke-on-Trent, Staffordshire; "& Son" added after 1871.)

$1,000+

French barn-shaped
covered tureen with chicken handles and hen with chicks on cover, good detail, unusual form, minor nicks, 8" long, 7" tall.

$700+

George Jones quail
game tureen with quail on lid with bed of wheat, pointed leaf and wheat base, minor rim nicks to interior rim of base, hairline crack to cover, 11" long. (Collector tip: The company started operations in the early 1860s as George Jones in Stoke, Staffordshire, England, and in 1873 became George Jones & Sons Ltd.)

$750+

Lavender covered
game tureen with liner, good color, professional rim repair to base and rim of lid, 9" wide.

$750+

Victoria Pottery Co.
boar's head game tureen with brown ground trimmed in green, insert included, minor nick to handle, good detail, 12" wide. (Collector tip: Victoria Pottery Co., Hanley, Staffordshire, England, 1895 to 1927.)

$200+

Victoria Pottery Co.
boar's head covered tureen with floral, leaf and vine motif on base, great color and detail, professional repair to one handle, 15" wide. (Collector tip: Victoria Pottery Co., Hanley, Staffordshire, England, 1895 to 1927.)

$700+

Wedgwood covered tureen
with grapes and vine in high relief on base and cauliflower on cover, with insert, 7 1/2" wide. (Collector tip: Founded by Josiah Wedgwood in 1759 at Burslem, Staffordshire, England.)

$450+

Wedgwood oriental floral
round covered tureen, rim repair to cover, hairline to base, 10" diameter.

$800+

Umbrella Stands

Umbrella stands are some of the largest and most elaborate pieces of majolica ever made, and prices for examples in good condition have risen sharply, even for those with restoration.

Fielding dead game

umbrella stand, tree trunk base with full bodied dead game hanging off of tree trunk including rabbit and mallard duck, fox glove flowers and leaves decorate tree stump, great detail, professional repair to duck bill and wing, 25" tall. (Collector tip: Railway Pottery, established by S. Fielding & Co., Stoke, Stoke-on-Trent, Staffordshire, England, 1879.)

$6,750+

Fielding turquoise

stork and bark umbrella stand, 22 1/2" tall.

$1,500

Holdcroft cobalt

water lily and bamboo umbrella stand, strong color, 23" tall. (Collector tip: Joseph Holdcroft majolica ware was produced at Daisy Bank in Longton, Staffordshire, England, from 1870 to 1885. Items can be found marked with "JHOLDCROFT" but many items can only be attributed by the patterns and colors that are documented to have come from the Holdcroft potteries.)

$3,250+

Vases and Flower Holders

Some majolica pieces listed here are valued in groups, and are representative of what a collector might find at large auction or private sale. Some pieces are grouped by color or style, others by use, and a few by manufacturer. The phrase "various conditions" is shorthand for a range of cracks, chips, flaking, repairs, crazing and staining. Rare or important pieces of majolica will usually have a provenance, and any repairs or restorations should be noted when they are sold.

Though assortments may offer limited information on the value of any single piece, they are an excellent place for beginning collectors to start gathering information on makers, marks, years of production and rarity.

Baltimore Pottery Co.
grape pattern vase with gryphon handles, 7" tall.

$120+

"BB" harvest lady
figural spill vase, nicks, 7 1/2" tall.

$60+

Blackamoor lady
figural vase, various repairs, 12" tall.

$100

Pair of terra-cotta
Blackamoor figural vases with man and woman with baskets, woman's head reattached, each 12" tall.

$400+ pair

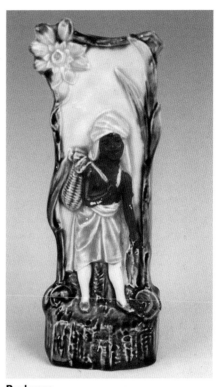

Brownfield ivy
and berry two-handled vase, minor hairline, 6 3/4" tall. (Collector tip: W. Brownfield & Son, Burslem and Cobridge, Staffordshire, England, 1850 to 1891.)

$150+

Brownfield pheasant
and rabbit figural vase, great detail, professional rim repair to leaves of vase, Bacall Collection, 14" tall.

$5,000+

Bud vase
with the figure of a Blackamoor, English, impressed "4842," 6 3/4" tall.

$170+

Courtesy the Iridescent House

Bud vase
with figure of a boy in military attire, English, impressed "4065," 6" tall.

$150+

Courtesy the Iridescent House

Bud vase
with figure of a boy holding a basket of apples, English, impressed "9619," 6" tall.

$250+

Courtesy the Iridescent House

Bud vase
with figure of a Chinaman, English, soft impressed number, 6" tall.

$175+

Courtesy the Iridescent House

Pair of Continental
figural Blackamoor floral vases, minor nicks, each 11 3/4" tall.

$450+ pair

Continental
figural vase of dog in red smoking jacket with pipe, 6" tall.

$100+

Continental
figural frog floral vase, 5" tall.

$90+

Pair of Copeland
cobalt mantle vases with floral and leaf motif, strong color and detail, each 11 1/2" tall. (Collector tip: William T. Copeland & Sons pottery of Stoke-on-Trent, England, began producing porcelain and earthenware in 1847.)

$2,750+ pair

Large figural owl
spill vase with large owl on tree stump and small owl on fence, good detail, base nick, 10" tall.

$400+

Forester stork
and cattail flower vase, professional repair to beak, 10 1/2" tall.

$8-$1,200

Pair of French
Art Nouveau two-handled floral vases, each 13" tall.

$250+ pair

French bird
and fruit figural vase, 12" tall.

$275+

Pair of French
figural lemon vases, artist signed "L Berty," one with professional rim repair, each 13 1/2" tall.

$700+ pair

Pair of French
figural ostrich vases, each 8 1/4" tall.

$125+ pair

French floral vase
with applied flowers, 8" tall.

$100+

Gerbing & Stefan
cobalt vase with butterfly, putti, flowers and insects in relief, hairline crack, chips, great detail, 10" tall.

$400

Delphin Massier
figural stork vase, good detail, 8 1/2" tall. (Collector tip: The Massier family began producing ceramics in Vallauris, France, in the mid-18th century.)

$350+

Delphin Massier pair
of small flower-shaped vases, minor glaze nicks, each 5" tall.

$200+ pair

Jerome Massier calla lily vase
good detail, minor glaze nick, 6" tall. (Collector tip: The Massier family began producing ceramics in Vallauris, France, in the mid-18th century.)

$425+

Pair of Massier-type
figural flower bud vases, minor nicks, each 8" tall.

$200+ pair

Minton vase

with basket-weave and applied floral motif, hairline, shape no. 1287, date code for 1870, good color, 6 3/4" tall. (Thomas Minton founded his factory in the mid-1790s in Stoke-on-Trent, Staffordshire, England. His son, Herbert Minton, introduced majolica pottery—with glazes created by Léon Arnoux—at England's Great Exhibition of 1851.)

$700+

Minton cobalt

mask vase, professional base and rim repair, 13" tall.

$1,500

Minton cobalt

and turquoise lily vase, shape no. 293, great detail, professional rim repair and base repair, 6 1/2" tall.

$200+

Minton French

figural lemon vase, good detail, 12" tall.

$400+

Minton French

figural lemon vase with twig handles, good detail, 6 3/4" tall.

$500+

Minton French
lemon and floral vase, chip to leaf, 6" tall.

$175+

Minton yellow
triple-hole bud vase with green ribbon and bow, 6" tall.

$6-$900

Royal Worcester
hand holding mottled flower vase, professional rim repair, rare form, 6" tall.

$4-$600

Rustic-style pitcher vase
English, 8 1/4" tall.

$700+

Courtesy the Iridescent House

Pair of Sarreguemines
dolphin and shell vases, shape no. 949, one with professional rim repair, 14 1/2" tall. (Collector tip: Named for the city in the Alsace-Lorraine region of northeastern France.)

$600+ pair

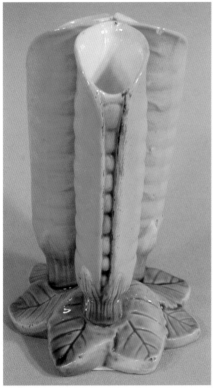

Triple-hole bud vase
of peas in pods, base repair, hairline crack, rim chip, 5 1/2" tall.

$50+

Vase
with figure of a girl holding her apron, English, soft impressed number, 10 3/4" tall.

$350+
Courtesy the Iridescent House

Vase
with transfer decoration of a boy and girl at play, origin unknown, raised mark, "732," 12 1/2" tall.

$1,200+
Courtesy the Iridescent House

Wedgwood mottled
hedgehog figural flower holder, scarce, 9" tall. (Collector tip: Founded by Josiah Wedgwood in 1759 at Burslem, Staffordshire, England.)

$600+

W.S. & S. vase
with mask feet and handles, 12 1/2", (Collector tip: Wilhelm Schiller and Sons, Bodenbach, Bohemia, established 1885.)

$500+

Wall Pockets

Vintage majolica wall pockets, even simple examples, are seldom found for under $100. Collectors should closely examine the area around the mounting holes for chips, cracks and repairs.

Czechoslovakia
bird wall pocket, 7" tall.

$120+

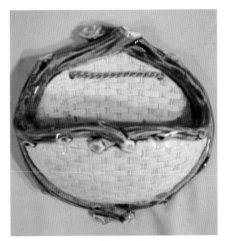

Etruscan basket-weave
and twig wall pocket, base chip, very rare, 6 1/4" tall, 6 1/4" wide. (Collector tip: Made by Griffen, Smith and Hill of Phoenixville, Pa., 1879 to about 1890.)

$4-$600

French dog
in basket wall pocket, 13" tall.

$300+

Delphin Massier rose
wall pocket, 9" long. (Collector tip: The Massier family began producing ceramics in Vallauris, France, in the mid-18th century.)

$350+

Wedgwood bird's nest
and bird wall pocket with fitted wooden back plate, strong color and detail, repair to bird and corner of bird's nest, rare, 12" wide, 9" tall. (Collector tip: Founded by Josiah Wedgwood in 1759 at Burslem, Staffordshire, England.)

$800+

Other Pieces

Some majolica pieces listed here are valued in groups, and are representative of what a collector might find at large auction or private sale. Some pieces are grouped by color or style, others by use, and a few by manufacturer. The phrase "various conditions" is shorthand for a range of cracks, chips, flaking, repairs, crazing and staining. Rare or important pieces of majolica will usually have a provenance, and any repairs or restorations should be noted when they are sold.

Though assortments may offer limited information on the value of any single piece, they are an excellent place for beginning collectors to start gathering information on makers, marks, years of production and rarity.

Ashtray
with matchbox holder, showing a jaguar killing a tapir, English, 8" long.

$250+
Courtesy the Iridescent House

Choisy-Le-Roi
large wishing well, 27" tall, strong color and detail, minor repair, atop Massier tree trunk pedestal, 26" tall. (Collector tip: The Choisy-le-Roi faience factory of Choisy-le-Roi, France, produced majolica from 1860 until 1910. The Massier family began producing ceramics in Vallauris, France, in the mid-18th century.)

$1,000+ pair

Bevington cat
with ball of yarn string holder, unusual form, professional repair to yarn on cat's paw, 6 1/4" tall. (Collector tip: The Bevington family of potters worked in Hanley, Staffordshire, England, in the late 19th century.)

$200+

Cobalt stork
and bamboo garden seat, strong color, hairline crack, attributed to Forester, 21" tall.
$2,000+

Continental smoke set
with checker board tray, dice humidor and match holder, two cigarette holders and poker chip striker, very unusual, various conditions.
$275+ set

Copeland shell
spoon warmer, porcelain with majolica colors, professional repair to rim of shell, 7" long. (Collector tip: William T. Copeland & Sons pottery of Stoke-on-Trent, England, began producing porcelain and earthenware in 1847.)
$275+

Etruscan water lily cuspidor
with white ground, hairline crack, chip.
$60+

Holdcroft cobalt
bird-footed glove box, great color, cranes in flight and flowers in relief, professional repair to foot, brass mounted hinged lid. (Collector tip: Joseph Holdcroft majolica ware was produced at Daisy Bank in Longton, Staffordshire, England, from 1870 to 1885. Items can be found marked with "JHOLD-CROFT," but many items can only be attributed by the patterns and colors that are documented to have come from the Holdcroft potteries.)
$2,000+

Holdcroft cobalt
covered square box with ball and claw feet, good detail and color, 8 1/4" wide.
$1,400+

George Jones "Briar" pattern
demitasse coffee server, not majolica. (Collector tip: The company started operations in the early 1860s as George Jones in Stoke, Staffordshire, England, and in 1873 became George Jones & Sons Ltd.)

$60+

George Jones turquoise
Neo-Classical hanging chandelier, vase and bottom plate/bowl of chandelier done in George Jones majolica, each is adorned with three ladies connected with pink ribbons and bows, grapes, vines and foliage, exquisite detail, repair to top rim of vase portion, majolica is attached to a cast brass five-light fixture with decorative rings, originally gas converted to electric, this appears to be an original factory made fixture, vase portion 14" tall, majolica plate/bowl, 12" diameter; 30" wide and 28" tall overall, extremely rare.

$10,000-$15,000

Hugo Lonitz partridges
with cattails under oak tree with oak leaves and acorns stand, strong color and detail, professional repair to oak leaves and cattail leaves, 13 1/4" tall. (Collector tip: Hugo Lonitz operated in Haldensleben, Germany, from 1868-1886, and later Hugo Lonitz & Co., 1886-1904, producing household and decorative porcelain and earthenware, and metal wares. Look for a mark of two entwined fish.)

$4,200+

Four majolica
and majolica-type pieces.

$40+ all

Minton turquoise wine cooler
with mythological mask and snake handles, strong color, shape no. 946, date code for 1871, 8 1/2" tall, 7 1/2" diameter. (Thomas Minton founded his factory in the mid-1790s in Stoke-on-Trent, Staffordshire, England. His son, Herbert Minton, introduced majolica pottery—with glazes created by Léon Arnoux—at England's Great Exhibition of 1851.)

$1,500-$2,000

Nine majolica
and majolica-type pieces, various conditions.

$60+ all

Reproduction bird
on leaf tray.

$10+

Three "sand" majolica items
various conditions.

$20+ all

St. Clement parrot decanter
12" tall. (Collector's tip: Founded by Jacques Chambrette in Saint-Clément, France, in 1758. Chambrette also established works in Luneville.)

$55+

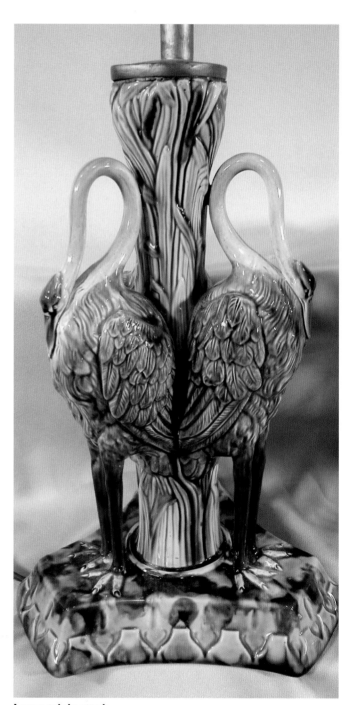

Large triple stork
and cattail table lamp, ceramic 11 1/2" tall.

$650+

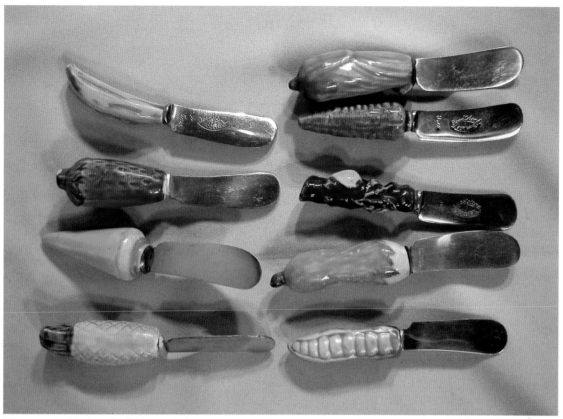

Nine vegetable-handled butter knives

$60+ all

Water lily marmalade pot
with attached under plate, interior rim chip, rim wear, staining.

$80+

Resources

Strawser Auction Group

200 N. Main St.

P.O. Box 332

Wolcottville, IN 46795-0332

(260) 854-2859

Fax: (260) 854-3979

http://strawerauctions.com/

info@strawerauctions.com

Joan Sween

Mom's Antique Mall

Highway 52 South

Oronoco, MN 55960

Mall: (507) 367-2600

Home: (507) 281-1472

sweens724@charter.net

Iridescent House, Inc.

227 First Ave. S.W.

Rochester, MN 55902

(507) 288-0320

http://www.iridescenthouse.com/

sales@iridescenthouse.com

Majolica International Society

PMB 103

1275 First Ave.

New York, NY 10021

http://www.majolicasociety.com/

secretary@majolicasociety.com

Maloney's Antiques & Collectibles Resource Directory:

Since its debut, Maloney's Antiques & Collectibles Resource Directory has been hailed as the "...best one-volume research tool in print." (Gannett News Service) and as a Best Reference Book (Library Journal.)

http://www.maloneysonline.com

Resources listed in Maloney's include:

* Buyers
* Collector Reference Book Sources
* Collectors
* Dealers
* Experts
* General Line and Specialty Auction Services
* Internet Resources
* Manufacturers and Distributors of Modern Collectibles
* Matching Services for China/Flatware/Crystal
* Overseas Antiques Tour Guides
* Regional Guides to Antiques Shops and Flea Markets
* Repair, Restoration and Conservation Specialists
* Reproduction Sources
* Specialty Collector Clubs
* Specialty Museums and Library Collections
* Specialty Periodicals
* Suppliers of Parts
* Trained Appraisers

Bibliography

American Majolica 1850-1900, M. Charles Rebert, Wallace-Homestead Book Company

Bernard Palissy: In Pursuit of the Earthly Paradise, Leonard N. Amico

Collecting Oyster Plates, Jeffrey B. Snyder, Schiffer Publishers, Ltd.

Collector's Encyclopedia of Majolica, Mariann Katz-Marks

European Majolica, D. Michael Murray, Schiffer Publishers, Ltd.

Figural Humidors, Mostly Victorian, Joseph Horowitz, M.D., FTJ Publications, Baltimore, Md.

George Jones Ceramics: 1861-1951, Robert Cluett, Schiffer Publishers, Ltd.

Les Barbotines, Pierre Faveton, Massin Editeur

Majolica Figures, Helen Cunningham, Schiffer Publishers, Ltd.

Majolica, Nicholas M. Dawes, Crown Publishers, Inc.

Majolica, Victoria Bergesen, Barrie & Jenkins, London

Majolica: A Complete History and Illustrated Survey, Marilyn G. Karmason with Joan B. Stacke. Harry N. Abrams, Inc.

Majolica: American and European Wares, Jeffrey B. Snyder and Leslie Bockol, Schiffer Publishers, Ltd.

Marvelous Majolica: An Easy Reference and Price Guide, Jeffrey B. Snyder, Schiffer Publishers, Ltd.

Oyster Plates, Vivian and Jim Karsnitz, Schiffer Publishers, Ltd.

Palissy Ware: Nineteenth-Century French Ceramists from Avisseau to Renoleau, Marshall P. Katz and Robert Lehr, The Athlone Press, London and the Atlantic Highlands, N.J.

Portuguese Palissy Ware: A Survey of Ceramics from Caldas Da Rainha, 1853-1920, Marshall P. Katz

Victorian Majolica, Leslie Bockol, Schiffer Publishers, Ltd.